JANE FONDA'S WORDS OF POLITICS AND PASSION

Also by Mary Hershberger

Jane Fonda's War: A Political Biography of an Antiwar Icon
Traveling to Vietnam: American Peace Activists and the War

JANE FONDA'S WORDS OF POLITICS AND PASSION

EDITED BY MARY HERSHBERGER

THE NEW PRESS

NEW YORK
LONDON

Requests for permission to reproduce selections from this book should be mailed to:
Permissions Department, The New Press, 38 Greene Street, New York, NY 10013.

Published in the United States by The New Press, New York, 2006
Distributed by W. W. Norton & Company, Inc., New York

Page xi constitutes an extension of this copyright page.

ISBN-13: 978-1-59558-131-0 (hc.)
ISBN-10: 1-59558-131-6 (hc.)
CIP data available.

The New Press was established in 1990 as a not-for-profit alternative to the large,
commercial publishing houses currently dominating the book publishing industry.
The New Press operates in the public interest rather than for private gain,
and is committed to publishing, in innovative ways, works of educational,
cultural, and community value that are often deemed insufficiently profitable.

www.thenewpress.com

Composition by dix!
This book was set in Bembo

Printed in the United States of America

2   4   6   8   10   9   7   5   3   1

Contents

Foreword

EVE ENSLER

If I have ever known any person willing to evolve, willing to learn, willing to change, willing to admit mistakes, willing to find a better way of doing something, it is Jane Fonda. She is what is called in Buddhist terms a seeking spirit. For me she has gone from being an icon to a close friend, from a movie star to a sister activist. We have traveled the world together: to Amman, Rome, Jerusalem, Mumbai, Mexico City, Juárez and throughout the United States, from the Pine Ridge Reservation in South Dakota supporting Native women to Los Angeles to stand with transgender women. I have watched her organize voting efforts and work with trade unions. I have marched with her. I have raised money with her. I have watched her build, step by step, a huge organization in Atlanta dedicated to empowering teenage girls and preventing early pregnancy. I have witnessed her literally change the lives of hundreds of women by publicly revealing her own vulnerability, mistakes and struggles.

Jane Fonda is an artist and an activist. Her commitment to transformation is total, imaginative and fierce. I have seen her lacerate an adulating press in Juárez for coming out to hear movie stars when they had remained silent for years in the face of the murder and disappearance of hundreds of Mexican women. I have seen her take broken, feisty teenage girls into her arms in a shelter in Jerusalem. I have witnessed her extreme generosity over and over—she changed my life and the lives of thousands by giving a million dollars to V-Day, a global movement to end violence against women and girls, which escalated the movement triple-fold.

From Jane I have learned about the power that is born at the intersection of art, politics and friendship. It is a new kind of power. It has to do with vulnerability. It has to do with asking questions.

Jane has shown me that if you speak truth to power, there will always be those who slander you and misconstrue you, protest you and try to reduce you. I have watched her weather attack after attack and remain unbitter and undefended. Oddly, it has strengthened her, making her clearer and more compassionate. From Jane I have learned that we must constantly seek a new and different way to communicate complicated ideas, that it is too easy to reduce people to positions or parties. That art can be active, can be political, can have a visceral impact, bringing transformation, conjuring revolution. Jane is proof that each of us can use our lives, our stature, our resources to serve something beyond ourselves. She has shown me that the struggle for justice, freedom, peace and equality is long, longer than you could have dreamed. It takes your life, but by taking your life, it gives you a life.

June 2006

Permissions

Introduction

Mary Hershberger

Jane Fonda's commitment to positive change has transformed her into one of the most visible and controversial figures of our time. Her witness against war, her environmental advocacy, her focus on health and fitness, and her work to secure fundamental rights of self-determination for women and girls around the world propelled her into the midst of sweeping social currents to a degree seldom exceeded. Indeed, Fonda's life has intersected with, and helped shape, significant social change in American life since the 1960s.

Fonda took on issues that other award-winning celebrities often shun for fear of alienating their fans. The price that she paid for her courage was scrutiny and defamation of outsized proportions. To a remarkable degree, the distinctive tactics that Jane Fonda's detractors developed decades ago to defame her have evolved into tactics standard in contemporary political defamation. Jane Fonda was "Swift-boated" decades ago—well before that peculiar operation was finally named during the elections of 2004.

Jane Fonda's life as an actress first put her in the public eye as a young woman, winning her wide acclaim that has included two Oscars and an Emmy, among numerous other awards and nominations. She could have followed the conventional life of a Hollywood celebrity and reaped even greater accolades. But she chose a life of engaged activism that gave voice to her values, even though she risked alienating her film audience. To the extent that the war in Vietnam remains a polarizing issue today, so does the name of Jane Fonda, who dispassionately jeopardized her award-winning acting career in 1970 to challenge that war directly, even traveling alone to the "enemy" country and declaring that the people there were no threat to the United States.

As a young adult, Fonda, like many of her generation, learned geography through America's interventions and wars: Korea, Lebanon, Iran, Guatemala, Dominican Republic, Cuba, Chile— and Vietnam. The McCarthy era had left many in Hollywood quiescent and Fonda, a self-described cynic then, knew little about Vietnam at first. But when she met antiwar GIs, visited wounded veterans and read eyewitness reports from the war, she was motivated to learn more and take action. "You can do one of two things: just shut up, which is something I don't find easy, or learn an awful lot very fast, which is what I tried to do," she said.

For five years, from 1970 to 1975, Fonda worked tirelessly to end the war in Vietnam, using her celebrity status to raise money— lots of it—for antiwar groups, especially for local organizing. She supported the off-base GI coffeehouses and created an entertainment revue, *Free the Army,* that drew crowds of wildly applauding GIs at venues in the United States and areas around military bases in the Pacific. With the help of sympathetic senators on Capitol Hill, she founded the GI Office in Washington, D.C., to provide free legal aid for young draftees and help them address grievances through their elected representatives in Congress. Through the GI coffeehouses, she funded the first counseling for veterans who suffered from post-traumatic stress disorder at a time when the army largely ignored the psychological costs that war imposed on them. The Federal Bureau of Investigation, the Central Intelligence Agency and the White House itself began to shadow her, taking her personal documents illegally and following her wherever she went.

Fonda's famed 1972 trip to Hanoi came amid alarming reports that the United States was bombing the dikes that held back the Red River in North Vietnam. In July, she traveled to Hanoi, armed with a camera and tape recorder, to investigate these reports. She returned with filmed evidence of the bombing (which the White House stiffly denied), but her film "disappeared" shortly after she returned to New York. Instead of images of bombed dikes that Fonda had gathered, the image of Fonda sitting on an antiaircraft emplacement, talking and laughing with the young Vietnamese crew around it, became the iconic image of that visit. Nonetheless, her trip to Hanoi heightened media attention to the bombing of the dikes and provoked an international outcry that ended it.

In Vietnam, Fonda had spent considerable time in air-raid shelters, sometimes lying in a ditch by the road as American bombers swooped over nearby towns and villages. The experience of living under bombs dropped by her own government was radicalizing—not only for Fonda but also for the hundreds of other American antiwar activists who had gone to Vietnam before she did. Seeing the bombers above her in the blue skies of Vietnam inspired Fonda to speak directly to the air crews of what she could see from her perspective on the ground below their planes.

Fonda's decision to speak of her own experiences over Radio Hanoi was in line with her focus on the personal throughout all of her advocacy. Decisions involving national issues of foreign policy are generally viewed as beyond the scope of personal appeals, but Fonda disregarded that convenient convention. In the United States, she had spoken against the war by invoking its individual and personal horrors. Now, in North Vietnam, she tape-recorded what she saw each day and then provided the tape to broadcasters at Radio Hanoi, who either aired the tapes as they were or translated them into the Vietnamese language and read the translations.

The Central Intelligence Agency made transcripts of Jane Fonda's Radio Hanoi broadcasts, some of which cycled through two translations and are not what Fonda herself recorded. This book only includes transcripts of broadcasts that Fonda made herself, in English, over Radio Hanoi.

Fonda's antiwar work continued unabated, even as American attention waned when the United States turned combat duties entirely over to the Vietnamese army which it trained. She objected to what she considered a cynical view in Washington that if the dead bodies were increasingly Vietnamese and not American, anxiety about the war would abate, ensuring Nixon's reelection. To that end, when she returned from Hanoi, she helped to organize the Indochina Peace Campaign to move the antiwar effort from a focus on street demonstrations and rallies to local communities and electoral work.

In 1974, Fonda went back to Vietnam and made one of the first films to document the ordinary lives of a so-called enemy from the perspective of friendship. She produced the film, *Introduction to the Enemy,* through IPC Films, an outgrowth of her Indochina Peace Campaign. It was a "quiet, modest film," in the words of critic Nora Sayre, that "stressed that the Vietnamese do not hate Americans, they want to know more about us." Fonda could have made an intensely political film, but in keeping with her consistent focus on the particular and the personal, she made an optimistic film that focused on the lives of ordinary people with inspiring themes of reconciliation, rebirth and rebuilding.

When the United States left Vietnam completely in 1975, Fonda used her newly acquired skills in fund-raising and organizing to raise money for the Campaign for Economic Democracy, an organization that she started with her then-husband, Tom Hayden. Opposition to nuclear power was one of the cornerstones of the campaign, and Fonda set out to make a film that raised those issues in a compelling fashion. The film that she made with Michael

Douglas and her producing partner Bruce Gilbert was called *The China Syndrome,* a title that Fonda liked but which some studio heads objected to at first, claiming that the idea of a nuclear meltdown so catastrophic that it threatened "to burn all the way down to China" was preposterous. But Fonda had already won two Oscars, and she and Douglas used their clout to insist on the title.

When *The China Syndrome* was released in March 1979, its tale of an attempted cover-up of a nuclear power plant accident and its depiction of graft, corporate greed, and feckless media bosses drew criticism. Conservative columnist George Will scolded Fonda and the other producers for needlessly scaring the public, but two weeks later a chilling accident at the nuclear power plant at Three Mile Island in Pennsylvania shocked the nation into breathless horror as people living around the power plant fled. *The China Syndrome* became a hit. As anti–nuclear-energy sentiment deepened, Fonda embarked on a nationwide tour, warning of the potential dangers that nuclear power plants posed. These events galvanized national opposition to nuclear energy so effectively that not a single nuclear power plant has been built in the United States since. The name of Fonda's film, *The China Syndrome,* has long since passed into the lexicon.

After the domestic upheavals created by the war in Vietnam, organizing energy within the United States shifted radically away from national politics and turned inward, to personal issues. Fonda tapped into that hunger for personal fulfillment to raise money for her political work and in the process turned her lifelong interest in health into a business that helped define the fitness trends of the 1980s. *Jane Fonda's Workout Book* and *Jane Fonda's Workout* video were instant runaway bestsellers. The video, designed to be used over and over again, single-handedly created a demand for VCRs that ensured the success of that heretofore struggling industry.

Fonda's workout books and videos were hits because they showed people working out together with infectious enthusiasm and energy. They sold by the millions, raising more money for the Campaign for Economic Democracy than Fonda had ever dreamed possible, while helping to turn the 1980s into a "fitness decade." Fonda was an encouraging fitness teacher, explaining each step and urging people to believe in themselves and to work hard enough to "feel" the result. In a burst of inspiration that referenced her political work as much as her work with physical fitness, she coined the phrase "feel the burn," meaning that one should invest in the action at hand "until you know it's going to make a difference."

In the 1990s, Fonda turned to global issues of women's and girls' economic development and empowerment. In a way, this marked a return to her focus during the war in Vietnam that called attention to the officials who set policies that harmed women and children of whom they knew little, in communities far away. After the war in Vietnam, as the United States moved away from international cooperation, Jane Fonda worked to encourage it. She began attending international conferences where she learned about the conditions in poverty-stricken countries, and those experiences inspired her to work on behalf of women and children in a rapidly globalizing world.

The first of these was the International Conference on Population and Development in Cairo, Egypt, in 1994, which Fonda attended as a goodwill ambassador for the United Nations Population Fund. In a speech to a standing-room-only crowd in one of the largest rooms there, Fonda warned of new threats to national security in the wake of the Cold War. She cited global environment problems and economic hardships that created communities without hope and told her audience that in a world in which "one billion people do not get enough food to function," it was time to take some of the money that had gone into the Cold War and use it to reduce conflict by improving the quality of life for everyone.

Fonda went to the Cairo conference with her mind on global environmental and population issues, but she had an experience there that informed and enlarged her focus: a tour through a desperately poor area in Cairo where children and adults scrounged for their daily food and where girls were married off early, uneducated and ill-prepared for life. It was a disturbing glimpse into the life of an impoverished community, but Fonda's activist, enthusiastic hosts took her to a new and innovative program in the midst of this poverty that included a bustling school where poor girls learned to read and write and develop life skills, as well as learn about their own reproductive health, while receiving strong encouragement to postpone marriage until they were adults.

Fonda returned to the United States inspired by the work of the Cairo activists to bring their ideas back to her hometown, Atlanta. After intensive consultations with health-care professionals, she founded the Georgia Campaign for Adolescent Pregnancy Prevention, which went beyond the standard focus on contraception to what Fonda called "above-the-waist issues": helping girls and young women make informed choices about pregnancy, family planning, reproductive health and raising children. "Hope is the best contraceptive," Fonda said.

Fonda's travel to Cairo and then her work with adolescent girls in Georgia pulled her into increased international work on behalf of girls and women around the world. She went to Beijing for the United Nations Fourth World Conference on Women, where she addressed a large audience and then spent the rest of her time listening to women from across the globe talk about the particular difficulties that women faced in their communities back home. Women made up half the world's population, worked two-thirds of the world's working hours, earned one-tenth of the world's income, owned less than one-tenth of the world's property and made up barely 10 percent of elected legislators. The Beijing conference pledged to improve those figures. Its organizers called upon everyone to make that possible by working to improve the lives of women, including ensuring their access to family planning, health care and women's rights, which, the conference declared, were *human rights* that nations and states could not override.

As part of that effort, Jane Fonda went to Nigeria in 2000 to film grassroots and government efforts to educate adolescent girls there. She walked into classrooms of girls in Nigeria who were enrolled in innovative projects to build self-confidence. The schools, locally conceived and managed, provided at-risk girls with quality education, reproductive health education and programs that empowered them to enter into relationships based on equality and mutual respect. Fonda's documentary from her Nigeria trip, *Generation 2000: Changing Girls' Realities,* debuted at a conference in New York called Beijing + 5 that was convened to assess progress toward the Beijing Conference's ambitious goals.

Fonda's speeches on her international work are imbued with awareness that achieving equality between men and women involves complex decisions that range from the most intimately personal to global issues decided in the boardrooms of the wealthy and powerful. The imbalance in power, in resources, in wealth and in human capabilities calls for shifts within individuals and families, communities, nations and the world itself. "You cannot alleviate poverty and you cannot create sustainable development if you don't improve the lives of women," Fonda has often said.

Over the decades, Jane Fonda has poured her abilities and energies into many issues. On one hand, this could appear to be the work of a woman with a short attention span, leaping from one issue to another, pursuing each and every one with an overflowing tank of energy and then moving on to a new one. But dig a little deeper and we discover that these issues are all connected, bound together by Fonda's consistent concern for the personal welfare of children and women, an insistence that the measure of public issues, even of war, be taken in the way that they impact the weakest—the "least of these."

Fonda's concern for the welfare of those who enter this world with few assets pervades all of her work. In Vietnam, she painted in vivid colors the enormous toll that the war took on families, on children, on communities with little besides their small homes and water buffalo. Her observant eye noticed details that others usually missed: how those who filled in the bomb craters on the dikes were women, working with wheelbarrows and baskets, spending their lives carrying enormous quantities of dirt to keep their fields and communities safe despite the inevitability of the next bomb ordered over their heads by distant men living far away in ease. Her film *Introduction to the Enemy* "seethes with small children," one reviewer wrote, calling the film "as much personal as political." The slide show she put together when she returned from Vietnam was filled with images of the impact of the war on women, and so she called it simply "Women in Vietnam." Likewise, when Fonda appealed to the American pilots to consider what they were bombing in areas below, invisible to them, she spoke of how the people they were bombing were not so different from your "grandmothers and grandfathers" back in the United States.

Another theme in these speeches is a strong belief in the possibility of positive change for individuals, communities and nations. Fonda had once been Barbarella, she liked to say, and if she could change, than anyone could: "As long as I'm changing, there's hope for me," she said. Having lived through deadening cynicism in the 1950s, Fonda took on the war in Vietnam in a manner that encouraged ordinary people to have faith in their ability to bring about growth in themselves and their nation. The realities of poverty, the disenfranchisement and oppression of women: education and action could change these things.

In addition, Fonda constantly paid attention to what could be learned through experience. It was her belief in the value of experience that took her to Hanoi to live under the bombs and into the slums of Cairo to share, even if briefly, in the lives of others. Experience is a great educator, and Fonda used her experience to educate herself and other Americans about realities far from home. "A lot of people come to hear me because I'm an actress," she acknowledged once, but the fact that crowds were drawn first to her speeches because of who she was didn't matter much to her. "What I care about is what they leave with," she said. What Jane Fonda's audiences left with was usually greater, more detailed information about the issue that she was addressing than they had ever heard in one place before. "Once you connect with the painful truth of something, you then *own* the pain and must take responsibility for it through action," she once said.

The goal of ushering in a better world through positive change, Fonda says, can be achieved only with the active support of men willing to abandon the rules of patriarchy for a life more balanced, more invested in the experience of relationship. The opposite of patriarchy, Fonda observes, is not matriarchy but democracy. War, with its roots in patriarchy, is one of the greatest destroyers of relationships and of democracy. The war in Vietnam continued drearily on long after its goals were abandoned as unrealizable, Fonda believes, because leaders in the United States linked their personal manliness to national omnipotence. The current leadership guiding the war in Iraq has learned little in the years since: "They would rather disappear from public life, as Lyndon Johnson did, than be blamed for premature evacuation," Fonda says. "Look at the macho posturing in relation to the Iraq war," she points out, quoting some of the better-known phrases of that war: " 'Bring 'em on,' 'Are you man enough?' 'I knew that my God was bigger than his.' The patriarchal 'mine's bigger-than-yours' paradigm and drive for control has the entire world tilted in dangerous imbalance," she adds, "damaging not only individual women, men and children, but entire peoples."

The speeches in this book follow Fonda over the decades as she lived her life as an actress and activist, urging the importance of women's education, the value of experience, the potential for positive change, and the centrality of relationship to understanding issues, whether they deal with poverty alleviation, the international rights of women, or ending war and its violence. Jane Fonda's words ring with confident assurance that change is possible, that time spent in the pursuit of equality and justice is time well spent and that the personal matters, even when global issues are discussed and agreements reached. "Feel the burn," she told her workout audiences—keep working for change until you know that it's going to make a difference.

JANE FONDA'S WORDS OF
POLITICS AND PASSION

Part I

Political Awakening

WHY A MOVIE STAR
BECAME A PEACE ACTIVIST

My involvement is recent. I was a dropout. I was cynical. I was one of those American people who didn't even read the newspaper because I said, "Why bother? What could I possibly do to change anything?"

A lot of that cynicism and numbness of the brain came from having gone to school during the McCarthy era. And I remember what that did to people, how that silenced people. How it split them apart. How it made them afraid to argue and debate. How it made our teachers not talk about what was going on in the country and the world.

I lived in France for seven years. I was away when people began to pull themselves out of the McCarthy era of silence and fear, when people began to protest and get involved in the civil rights movement and the peace movement.

And I remember when I lived in France and the peace movement really started to gather momentum, all over French television one would see tens of thousands of American people in the streets protesting the war. And I remember how astonished I was to see how changed things had gotten here. And it was the people in the streets of America who forced me to think about Vietnam.

"Why Famous Actress Became a Peace Activist," *Philadelphia Bulletin*, October 1, 1972.

And it was the soldiers who deserted Vietnam—who left and said it was wrong. And how hard for them to say something like that.

I, at first, resisted. I said, "It's not true, Americans don't do things like these people are saying we're doing there."

And then I studied. It was the time of the Bertrand Russell war crimes tribunal, which I read carefully. And I talked to soldiers. And I came back to the United States and I realized that what we are told and what is actually happening in Vietnam are very, very different. And it was a very difficult thing for me. And I understand why it's difficult for Americans to say, "We're being lied to."

So I came back here. I'm a latecomer to the peace movement. But I'm very grateful for people who have protested and made it possible for me to open my mind to what's going on in Vietnam.

I wasted thirty-two years of my life. I'm going to be thirty-five in December. I know how important it is for people to be aware of what's going on. I know that when women get active—and it tends to happen to women more often because we are put into cubbyholes—we are told, like it said in the paper about my being in Kensington yesterday, "Why doesn't she go back and be content at being a housewife?"

I was a housewife for seven years. And I was like a leaf that dried up on a branch. I was defined by my husband. I was defined by the roles that I played in movies. My hair wasn't even my own color. I was defined in many, many different ways. And I know what that does to human beings.

And I believe that the struggle in Vietnam is very related to what happened to me as a woman. It is a struggle, I think, for everything that is human and good in the world that's being fought out there on the soil of Vietnam.

And it's just very important for me to say that because a lot of people think that the only reason I do what I do is because I'm famous. But I wouldn't be doing what I'm doing if people who are not famous hadn't made me start thinking about it.

FROM FANTASY TO
RADICALISM

I've been trying, over the last few years, to figure out why it took me so long to put the pieces together. I think part of it has to do with the fact that I grew up and went through the student years in the '50s. And what I remember about those times is very colored and conditioned by the fact that it was the McCarthy era. I remember this sort of overhanging sense that the movements for social change, protest, were fraught with danger, met with repression. I remember teachers in certain schools that I went to that were relatively progressive who were not around very long. I remember having to sit around a radio in boarding school the day that Stalin died having to applaud. We were never told why.

My father was always progressive. He would get worked up about McCarthy and what that meant to the country. Yet, that kind of liberalism within the family never did provide me with an alternative. I grew up feeling, "what's the use?"

One day, I suddenly remembered the first day I went to Warner Brothers when I was doing my first film there and they were examining my face. It was a bunch of expert makeup artists looking me over and it wasn't what they wanted. When they got finished

"Jane Fonda Looking Back: From Fantasy to Radicalism," *Washington Post,* July 29, 1972.

with me I didn't really know who I was. My eyebrows were like eagle's wings and my mouth was coming all over my face. My hair was not the right color and it had to be changed. Then Jack Warner, the head of the studio, sent a message to the set that I had to wear falsies because you couldn't become a movie star unless you were full-breasted.

It seems silly today, given the consciousness that exists, that I would accept that. But I just assumed these men were experts. So I allowed myself to be changed. What it does is completely alienate you from yourself and you spend your whole time pretending to be somebody other than yourself; not just on the screen, but because that is the standard that is being laid out for you as a woman as to what you're supposed to look like all the time. . . .

In '68 you had to deal with it. If you were in Paris, Paris was up in arms. Most everyone I knew was in the streets. Everything was changing overnight. I didn't have any political understanding of what was going on, except that people were moving. And people were moving in Chicago. The most specific thing I can remember was watching television when there was a march of half a million people on the Pentagon. That had a profound effect on me, because I suddenly realized to what degree the country had changed since I'd been away. I watched women walking up to the bayonets that were surrounding the Pentagon and they were not afraid. It was the soldiers who were afraid. I will never forget that experience. It completely changed me. It began my searching for what was behind it all. My place was not as a married woman in a household in a farm in France. . . . I wanted to find some way that I could be part of what was going on. For the first time in my whole life I realized that people were finding a way to create change. I didn't know what it was, all I knew was that people were beginning to feel powerful again. I wanted to be part of it. . . .

I went to talk to the Indians there [on Alcatraz Island] and realized, of course, that when you're a movie actress if you go anywhere where people are in trouble, you have to be an expert. I showed up at Alcatraz and suddenly the newspapers were all over the place and they wanted to know what I thought. I didn't know what I thought. I had only just arrived.

It was just prior to, and during, the Cambodian invasion and it was a hell of a time to drive across the country. I didn't realize there was this much motion. I'm aware, as we all are, of racism and poverty and unemployment. What I had not realized was how some things are tied together. I did visit some Indian reservations and time and time again I would see some white corporation heads lying to the Indians, wheeling and dealing to take their land away. I saw guys who will probably never be the same. You read about the post-Vietnam syndrome. I've seen hundreds of men suffering from it. They talk in whispers. Guys who would whisper in my ear that they were incapable of doing anything except perhaps killing. . . .

You suddenly open up the floodgates and you have no words to express what it is you're feeling. I mean, there were a lot of words that I just was beginning to understand what they meant. I borrowed a lot of rhetoric from a lot of people to try to give train-rails to what it was that I was feeling. And as a result, I was criticized and condemned for being all kinds of things. I was just trying to find a way to express what I was feeling—rage, rage that people feel when they've been lied to and suddenly realize it. Rage of someone who was, to a certain degree, despite the cynicism, very idealistic about my country and was very angry about the deception. Just anger—so angry. It comes from inexperience, it comes from not being part of an organization, it comes from working alone, it comes from being famous and easily backed into a corner. It comes from being a woman.

FINDING POLITICS IN FILM

Lord David Puttnam, producer of Chariots of Fire, The Killing Fields, *and* The Mission, *talks to Jane Fonda about four decades in the movies.*

LORD PUTTNAM: Good evening. I don't know how many of you have read the book [Jane Fonda's *My Life So Far*]. Or, like me, have heard Jane reading it on the radio this week. I thought it was a completely remarkable book and that it, in a sense, redefines autobiography because it has an honesty and frankness that people in the future are going to find it difficult to match. I was looking for a way of describing it and came across this Nobel Prize speech by Solzhenitsyn, and he uses a phrase which to me perfectly summed up the book: "It is useless to assert what one's heart does not believe." It seems to me that, sometimes with great pain, you've gone right through this book asserting exactly what your heart believes, and has learned to believe. And that's why it's a journey, not an autobiography—I felt like I'd been on a journey with you. What I'd like to do, because I've become pretty familiar with a lot of the book, and this being a rather more anoraky audience, is to concentrate on the movie industry aspects. And if I may, concentrate espe-

"Jane Fonda," *Guardian*/National Film Theatre Interview, *The Guardian,* June 3, 2005.

cially on a ten-year period in your career between 1969 and '79, from *They Shoot Horses, Don't They?* through to the completion of *The China Syndrome.* Where it seems to me that your choice of material was immaculate, and the way in which your life was bouncing between what was going on and the movies you were making, and how these movies in turn were affecting your life, was, I think, exemplary. One of the reasons why I'd like to do this is because I'm not sure that we're living in an era in cinema where that's necessarily true. I think it's certainly true that I and the people I was working with in the 70s and 80s were learning an enormous amount by what you were doing and achieving and the way you were living your life and the way you were using the metaphor of cinema to make points which badly needed to be made.

One of the key films for me—and I went through Jane's oeuvre in the past week—was, and I didn't expect this when I started, *Coming Home.* It falls pretty well in the middle of that period, and I think it's a superb movie. If it were made yesterday it couldn't be more relevant. And so tonight I'm using two clips from that, including the one we've just seen [Sally and Luke's first date]. So I'd like to start with *They Shoot Horses,* and the events that led up to you getting that part, what you learned from that role, and what you feel it did for you in terms of feeding your career from that point onwards.

JANE FONDA: Well, it was a book written by Horace McCoy, sort of the first existential American novel, that was very much loved by the French left. My husband at the time, Roger Vadim, knew the book. When I was offered the role—it was not a very good script, and I said no, and he said, "No, you have to do this," so I did. And I'm glad I did. Because soon after I accepted the role and arrived to do it, the original writer-director was fired and this young Sydney Pollack—who had only done one other feature film prior to that, but had become famous in television in the US—was hired to direct it.

The first really seminal moment was when he came to my rented house and he brought the book with him. He sat down and said, "I want you to read the book and I want you to tell me what you think are the key elements in it that need to be brought out in the film." Doesn't seem like a big thing to you, maybe, but nobody had ever asked me to really participate in the content of a movie that I was in before. This was 1968—it was a very tumultuous time, a time of a lot of change. The movie I'd made before that was *Barbarella*. So it's interesting to go, in the year 1968, from *Barbarella* to *They Shoot Horses, Don't They?*

Phew! And I was also morphing from a noun into a verb. And the movie of *They Shoot Horses* was kind of the beginning of my being a verb. And the fact that Sydney asked me what I thought was part of that process. It's very important to me—I work with young people now and I learned from that experience with Sydney the importance of asking children's opinions, and really listening to them. At any rate, it was the first time I'd done a movie that was relevant to what was happening in the world. The marathon dances of the Depression were a metaphor for American consumer society that was killing our souls, and I'd never done anything like that before.

LP: For me, just looking at the films that ran up to it, there is a transformation in you, as an actor. Here's a clip from early on in *They Shoot Horses.*

[Runs clip where Gloria and Robert start dancing and make conversation]

JF: Man, she was a tough . . .

LP: She was one tough girl. I think that line, "I've been disqualified by experts," is sensational. Pauline Kael, when reviewing the film, said, "Jane Fonda has been a charming, witty, nudie cutie in recent years, and now gets a chance at an archetypal character. Fonda goes all the way with it, in a way that screen actresses rarely do once they become stars. Jane Fonda has a good chance of personifying American tensions and dominating our movies in the 70s." Pretty prescient review—they don't always get it as right as that.

JF: Good old Pauline Kael.

LP: But it did represent an enormous step change. To what extent did that segue quite naturally into *Klute*?

JF: I had just finished making it when I was offered the role of Bree Daniel in *Klute*. It seemed like a really good idea. A year went by between my agreeing to do it and when I actually did it, and during that year I was traveling around the United States, trying to understand the country because I'd been living in France since I married Roger Vadim. I'd been out of the country for eight years. How long should this answer be? I could talk a lot about this film.

LP: Well, it's a pretty important film.

JF: I'll tell you a funny part of it. So the production manager had arranged for me to spend time with prostitutes and madams prior to shooting. So I did that, I went to New York. I didn't look like I was supposed to because I'd been Barbarella and now I had this short, brown shag that became famous in *Klute*. Nobody knew who I was. I could tell some pretty good stories about what they told me and what I saw—man, it was wild. And the whole time, I would be going to these after-hours clubs, and no pimp would pick me up. Not even a wink. They didn't know who I was, so what that said to me was that I was wrong for the part, I just didn't have what it took. So I begged Alan Pakula to fire me, I said, "I can't do it, Alan," and gave him a list of actors, starting with Faye Dunaway— I said, "She should do it." And he just laughed and I did it.

Somewhere in there, I just . . . and it was the first movie I did where I experienced this: there was like a marriage, a melding of souls between this character and me, this woman that I didn't think I could play because I didn't think I was call girl material. It didn't matter. I didn't know until I was writing the book why. I knew women like her, very talented—she could have been a very good actor. But she'd been abused when she was a child, so she wanted to be in control. And she didn't want intimacy, and hooking was a great way to get money for acting classes and she would always be in control—because hookers are in control, except when they're killed. I studied the effects of child abuse on girls. Originally, a male psychiatrist had been hired, and I said, "Alan, it can't be a male, she would never open up to a man." So he put a woman in the role. And all those scenes were improvised, because by then I had inhabited her, and I knew why she hooked, why she wanted johns, I knew it in my skin. And of course I realize there was a lot of me there, but I didn't know it at the time.

LP: There's a very early scene in that: the lineup for the modeling job that you go for, of twelve to fourteen girls. And the coldness, the sense of absolutely unjustifiable rejection, sets up the film brilliantly. You can't understand it, why would anyone put themselves up for that kind of rejection and not be badly damaged by it. Brilliant start. The clip I've chosen, ironically, is one of the scenes where Jane is talking to the psychiatrist, and I didn't know that it was . . . Did you agree with Alan going in that you would ad-lib those scenes?

JF: Uh-huh.

LP: Perfect. We chose well.

[Runs clip: Bree talks to psychiatrist about why she's a call girl]

JF: There was a turning point for me in that movie. It was toward the end of the movie, when I find myself with a john, and he puts on a tape recorder. On the tape is the voice of my friend, a junkie who's disappeared and we don't know where she is. And in the course of listening I realize that the man is the one who killed her and he's going to kill me. Prior to that scene, I had asked Alan to arrange for me to go into the New York City morgue. And the police showed me file after file after file of women, hundreds of them, who'd been beaten to death, by johns, by husbands, by boyfriends. I knew about violence against women but I hadn't realized. . . . It had flesh and bones to it now, it had faces. And that scene, where I'm listening to the tape and realizing that this man is going to kill me, I had decided not to prepare. I have a hard time acting fear. So I was just going to listen, because I'm a good listener. And what happened to me was I felt so sad, for all of us, for women, who are so vulnerable to the misplaced anger of men, so vulnerable that it seemed so inevitable that we were all beaten and bloodied and killed and it was going to happen to me, and I began to cry. I was crying for women, and tears were coming out of my nose; it was a very affecting scene that had an effect on people. I didn't think it would at the time. But when the scene was over, I knew something new about myself as an actor. I knew that my newfound activism and feminism was going to improve my acting, because I was now seeing things not just in very narrow, individual, kind of Freudian terms, but seeing them in a much broader, societal way that was going to deepen and enrich my talent. And that was the moment that it happened. It was a very important time for me right then.

LP: I think the core of my thesis for this evening is the degree to which the interests you were developing, and the life you were beginning to lead, were beginning to seriously impact material which you chose to involve yourself with, and indeed the films that got made that just absolutely would not have been made had you not thrown yourself into them, *Coming Home* being one. It's this synthesis that interests me a lot. Can you develop that at all?

JF: Well, studios weren't banging on my door to offer me parts. And I was working really hard to try and end the war. I thought, it takes three months to make a feature film and I just couldn't imagine spending three months making a film just for the money. And I thought, well how am I ever going to make movies that speak to my heart and to my values? So I was at an antiwar rally with a guy in a wheelchair named Ron Kovic. Maybe some of you saw Tom Cruise play his story in *Born on the Fourth of July*. Ron, very fiery, very charismatic, had been real gung-ho; he re-enlisted for three terms in Vietnam, had been shot and was paralyzed from the waist down and was in a wheelchair. I was speaking at the same rally, and I heard him say—he was talking to students—he said, "I may have lost my body but I've gained my mind." That, I don't know, that just kind of pierced me, entered me. For weeks, I kept thinking of that contradiction: he had lost his body but he had come to understand that the war was wrong. He had come to shed the traditional warrior ethic to become a full human being. And I said, we could make a movie about that, and that's what evolved into *Coming Home.*

LP: When Patsy and I watched the film, she said she saw Ron Kovic in a relatively small part in the film. Was he there?

JF: Could have been—we had a lot of vets in wheelchairs. Can I talk about the sex part of it?

LP: If you insist.

JF: Well, I don't know; how much time do we have?

LP: In my experience, we've got enough time to deal with sex.

JF: Somewhere along in there, I thought, because it was becoming clear that this was becoming a love story: a triangle between a woman who was an officer's wife—and he was the kind of real gung-ho, I'm-gonna-go-I'm-gonna-be-a-hero; Bruce Dern played that part—and Jon Voight, who doesn't have the bottom part of his body. A love story. And I thought, maybe this is a way to redefine sexuality, sensuality; away from the traditional genitalia and masculinity and pumping, and make it be about what women know really matter, which is when the man is really sensitive to what we need and listens to our bodies and pays attention to us because they want to please us. And I thought, well this would be a great way to not only expose what's happening to Vietnam vets but to redefine sexuality. The problem was that . . . there were a lot of these guys in wheelchairs on the set, extras on the film, and there was this guy who had a really cute girlfriend and there was clearly a lot of sexual energy between them. So I asked them about the sex between them because we had this love scene coming up and I didn't know how you do it with somebody who's paralyzed. So she said, "You never know when he's going to get an erection. It can be anytime, and sometimes it lasts four hours." Phew! I was totally fascinated by it but I was also kind of disappointed because I was hoping that it wasn't possible because then it would be a movie where there was no penetration. The problem was that the director, the fabulous Hal Ashby, also heard the story about the four hours. And so the movie became the battle of penetration. He wanted to have the penetration and I didn't. Can I just finish off?

LP: I wish you would. Put it in another way, I'd never be forgiven if you didn't.

JF: We knew it had to be a really sexy and groundbreaking kind of scene. And I didn't want to have to do it myself so we got a body double to shoot the long shots. And I didn't want to make Jon Voight self-conscious, so I wasn't there when they shot with the body double. I came to the rushes the next day, and there was definitely penetration—she was moving on top of him, it was pretty clear what was going on. I said, "Hal, you can't use that! I thought we agreed." And then I thought, aha, when it comes to shooting my close-ups, I won't move, so he won't be able to cut it in. And so the day of the love scene—it's always interesting to shoot love scenes: they're skin on skin, and they hang sheets. I don't know if you did this in your films, but I'm kind of modest, so they hung sheets around, and there's only the camera operator and the director who are sort of there with long lens cameras. We spent the day rolling around in bed, and trying to say, "It's OK, it's only acting," right? And so towards the end of the day, I'm on top of Jon, and I hear Jon saying to me, [stage whispering] "Jane, Hal's yelling at you." And I was so into the scene that I hadn't heard. But suddenly, I listened and from the distance, I hear Hal Ashby saying, "Ride him, goddammit!" I refused, I wouldn't do it, and he stormed off the set. Right now, you can't really tell—some people think it's penetration, some people don't—but for the day, it was really a hot scene, wasn't it?

LP: My only experience of this was—and this might end up selling a lot of videos of a film that no one's ever seen—I produced a really execrable film in the mid-70s called *Lisztomania,* and I hope that no one here's seen it. It had Roger Daltrey and a very, very nice girl called Fiona Lewis in an early scene. And all they had to do was lie in bed underneath a silk sheet. And Ken Russell, who's not the easiest person to produce, was directing everything else that was going on around them. But they lay there for hours. And it was just before lunch, and Ken suddenly got it into his head, "I wonder if we can do it without the sheet"; and he whipped the sheet back and there was silence.

JF: They were getting it on!

LP: Well, I didn't know we were going to go there. So, *Coming Home.* Here's another clip I'd like to show which I think is sensational. I think this is really exquisite acting. You mentioned that a lot of this also was improvised. So another improvised scene from *Coming Home,* but which I think is fabulous.

[Runs clip: Sally and Luke on the beach on the eve of her husband's return]

JF: You know, what's so striking is that nowadays movies don't let scenes play out like that. You don't find movies anymore that sort of take the time to let it happen. It's so great for an actor to be able to do that.

LP: It's absolutely true—Jane and I first met at the pre-Oscar party the year that she won for that performance, and you were very, very gracious to a very nervous Alan Parker and I. But when you think of that year, the films nominated for best film were *Coming Home, The Deer Hunter,* which won, *An Unmarried Woman* and *Midnight Express.* It's hard to imagine that level of seriousness happening today. And I guess one of the things that's driving me throughout this is how can we get back to that, how can we get back to films that will allow that to happen on the screen. I'd like to talk to you about Vietnam for a moment because you are so eloquent about it in the book; the passages on Vietnam are wonderful. I wonder if you could both read that very short paragraph and talk a little about that.

JF: Oh yes, I'm in Hanoi, out in the country. I had visited a city that had been bombed, and we were on our way back. We were maybe an hour outside Hanoi, and bombing was taking place. I was told that I had to get out of the car and run because the bombers were coming. So I did, with my translator, and we ran. All along the side of this road at regular intervals were these manholes for individual people that had thick straw lids that you pull over to protect you from the bombs and the shrapnel. So I was running and suddenly a young Vietnamese girl comes up behind me and pulls me down into one of these holes. She was a schoolgirl, she had her books wrapped up in a belt. She dropped them and pushed me down into this hole and then she got into the hole with me and pulled the top on. And then shortly thereafter you could hear the planes overhead and you could feel the bombs thudding, thudding, thudding. It was very small and we were sandwiched in together—I could feel her breath, and her eyelashes, on my cheek. I swear to God, I thought, this can't be real. I can't be in a manhole in Vietnam with a Vietnamese girl who's just saved my life. It's not possible. When the bombing raid was over, she pushed the top over and crawled back out, and I came out, and this is where I'll begin to read now: "I began to cry, saying over and over to the girl, 'I'm sorry. I'm so sorry. I'm so sorry.' She stops me and starts speaking to me in Vietnamese. Not angry, very calm. Huoc—he's the translator—translates. 'She says you shouldn't cry for us. We know why we're fighting. The sadness should be for your country, your soldiers. They don't know why they are fighting us.' I stare at her and she looks right back, right into my eye. Certain."

LP: Last autumn, I worked with Unicef and Patsy and I were in Hanoi for the first time. And I walked into a hotel and bumped into a group of people I'd known at Warner Bros., guys my age. And I said, "Have any of you been here before?" And they all said, "The last time we were in this country, we wouldn't have been as welcome." And they'd all been GIs, and what struck them, as I'm sure has struck you many, many times since, was how ludicrous the entire Vietnamese adventure was. Here they were in a very nice hotel in a rapidly becoming prosperous city. And none of them could work out, for one moment, what that war had been about. Domino theory, none of it made any sense at all.

JF: Yeah, the so-called Enemy One, and we're big export-import traders with Vietnam; it's one of the key destinations. A tragedy that never had to happen. I hope I'm going to be able to see Robert McNamara—he's going to be in Hay-on-Wye. I really admire the fact that he admitted that it was wrong.

LP: I don't know if many of you have seen *Fog of War*—if you haven't seen it, it's well worth seeing, the McNamara documentary. Remarkable document, actually.

JF: I saw it back-to-back with *The Trials of Henry Kissinger*. Talk about two different kinds of human beings. I mean, McNamara was one of the architects of the Vietnam war; how hard, what courage it took for him to finally say, "We were wrong." Boy. You don't find Kissinger doing that.

LP: The penultimate clip that I've chosen doesn't have Jane in it, but I think has enormous resonance and is touched on in the book and you even use it as a sort of chapter heading. It's from *The Grapes of Wrath*. For those at home watching the webcast, I do apologize but you won't see it. Instead of which you may well see a photograph of Rupert Murdoch, who decided that we shouldn't be allowed to webcast this particular set of images. So sorry about that. It's three minutes and thirty-five seconds long, so if you're at home, go and make a cup of tea and we'll be right back with you.

[Runs clip: Tom Joad's "I'll be there" speech]

LP: That's one of my favorite scenes from any movie, but I think that's a series of thoughts that run right the way through this book, from cover to cover. You're constantly, in a way, circling exactly that group of thoughts.

JF: Yes, it's true. I believe it's true, and I know that my father lives on in that same way. I know one of Martin Luther King Jr.'s daughters, Yolanda King. And while I was writing this book, she called me about something one day, and I had been thinking a lot about my father, and I asked her, "Yolanda, did your father ever take you on his lap when you were a little girl and talk to you about values and how to live life?" And she said, "No, he never did." I said, "Yeah, my dad never did either, but you have his sermons, and I have my dad's films. This is how he speaks to me. Not everyone can verbalize, right? I feel so blessed that I had a father that chose these kinds of roles—*Young Mr. Lincoln, Grapes of Wrath, Ox-Bow Incident.* There was a dialectic between him and those characters that spoke to me.

LP: Would you read that—it's the last thing I'll ask you to read, I promise.

JF: This is . . . my dad died, and I'm talking about being in his home with his widow and my family: "We'd sit together and watch his eulogies on television. All week they went on, and it hit me that this wasn't just my loss, the family's loss. It was a national loss. Dad was a public figure, a hero who didn't just belong to us. Dad lived out these quintessential American values. He represented things that we all wanted to be, and that the country wanted to be. He often said that he was attracted to certain kinds of roles—the working poor, powerless people and the men who helped them get some power for themselves—because somehow their characters might rub off on him, and he would become a better person. But now I saw that there had been a dialectic. He did have many of those qualities."

LP: The interesting thing for us in the UK, certainly for anyone who's my age, is that he didn't just have it for Americans, he represented something that's very, very fundamental and very, very important, and he's left a gap. It means that if you're like, in your sixties, you're scratching constantly for a notion of what's good that isn't around you. And I certainly feel this terrible vacuum that's been created between the ideals that your father was able to beautifully expound, and the pretty tatty, tawdry world that most of us are forced to deal with.

JF: I see it all the time. It's just not represented in our leaders but it's in the people. I feel particularly optimistic now because I've been traveling for five weeks now to promote my book, through the so-called red states. I tell you what, there's a lot of blue in those red states, and a lot of red in the blue, which means that we're all basically purple. Anyway, 800–900 people would come to the book signings, and I'm very optimistic. They represent the values my father stood for.

Part II

Against War

When Fonda visited Hanoi in 1972, the CIA recorded her broadcasts over Radio Hanoi and prepared the following transcripts.

DIKES IN
THE RED RIVER DELTA

July 14, 1972, broadcast, after Fonda visited Nam Sach district, about thirty miles east of Hanoi.

Yesterday morning [words deleted by CIA], I went to the district of Nam Sach to see the damage that has been done to the dikes in that district. And I wondered what has been going on with the hands of those who were pulling the levers and dropping the bombs on the fields and on the dikes of the Red River Delta. Do you know, for example, that for centuries since the middle ages, the Vietnamese peasants have built up and reinforced a great complex network of dikes which hold back the torrential water of the rivers flowing down from the mountains in summer during the monsoon seasons? Without these dikes, fifteen million people's lives would be endangered and would die by drowning and by starvation.

Anthony Lewis from the *New York Times* wrote an article just before I left the United States in which he said that successive U.S. administrations had rejected the idea of bombing the dikes in the Red River Delta because they all felt the dikes are not entirely military targets and that this was the type of terrorist activity that was unworthy of American people and American flags. But today, as you know better than I, American phantom jets are bombing strategic points in the dike networks in this area.

I beg you to consider what you are doing. In the area where I went yesterday it was easy to see that there are no military targets, there is no important highway, there is no communication network, there is no heavy industry. These are peasants. They grow rice and they rear pigs. They are similar to the farmers in the Midwest many years ago in the U.S. Perhaps your grandmothers and grandfathers would not be so different from these peasants. They are happy people, peace-loving people. When I went by walking on the way to the dikes to see the damage . . . I was afraid of the reaction that would be taken by the local people. But they looked at me curiously and I saw no hostility in their eyes . . . They seemed to be asking themselves: what kind of people can Americans be, those who would drop all kinds of bombs, so carelessly on their innocent heads, destroying their villages and endangering the lives of these millions of people?

All of you in the cockpits of your planes, on the aircraft carriers, those who are loading the bombs, those who are repairing the planes, those who are working on the 7th fleet, please think what you are doing. Are these people your enemy? What will you say to your children years from now who may ask you why you fought the war? What words will you be able to say to them?

RUINS OF NAM DINH

July 19, 1972, broadcast, after Fonda went to Nam Dinh, North Vietnam's third-largest city.

I was taken to all parts of the city. I saw with my own eyes that in this city which is the textile capital of Vietnam, there are no military targets. I saw for example, on Hang Tien Street, bombing on the 23rd of June, huge bomb craters which had destroyed houses in this very populated residential section of town. There were two women who were picking through the rubble left by the bombs and they came over and spoke to me. One of the women said that she'd been at the market when the bomb fell on the top of her house. Her house has been turned into a huge bomb crater. Her husband and three children were all killed. Her oldest son was twenty-five years old, her next oldest son had been twenty-two, and her youngest son was eighteen. Three families in this area were entirely destroyed by the bombs.

As I walked through the streets, beautiful Vietnamese girls looked at me through the doors and returned my smile. Their eyes seemed to be questioning: How is it that the Americans can do this to our city? We have done nothing to them.

I saw a secondary school where 600 students from fifth to seventh grade had been in class. That school had been hit by two bombs. I saw the center of a Chinese residential district, bombed, three planes, houses razed to the ground.

The number one hospital of the city which had two hundred beds and treated people from all over the city—large parts of it had been destroyed, particularly the pediatrics department and the supply department where the medicines had been kept.

The large factory, the textile factories of Nam Dinh are in charred ruins. No one is allowed to go in there because there are delayed reaction bombs.

I went to the dike system of the city of Nam Dinh. Just this morning at four o'clock it was bombed again, and I was told that an hour after we left the city, planes came back and re-bombed Nam Dinh. The dike in many places has been cut in half and there are huge fissures running across the top of it.

Again, I am talking about these things and I am describing to you what I am seeing on the ground because I think that you must not understand that the destruction is being caused to civilian populations and residential areas, to cultural centers. I saw the pagodas bombed in Nam Dinh. The area in which there are theaters where people come to rest, the recreation centers were all destroyed in Nam Dinh.

What are your commanders telling you? How are they justifying this to you? Have you any idea what your bombs are doing when you pull the levers and push the buttons?

Some day we're going to have to answer to our children for this war. Some day we are going to have to explain to the rest of the world how it is that we caused this type of suffering and death and destruction to a people who have done us no harm. Perhaps we should start to do it now before it is too late.

Perhaps, however, the most important thing that has to be said about Vietnam is that despite all that Nixon is doing here and that Johnson has done before, despite all the bombs, the people are more determined than ever to fight.

Take Nam Dinh, for example. There are people who are still living in Nam Dinh. Their factories have been dispersed and they are still working. There is still electricity. People are going about their business.

Perhaps the most important thing that can be said about Vietnam at this time is that in spite of, or perhaps because of, the bombs and the destruction that has been caused by the Nixon administration and was caused by the Johnson administration before him to Vietnam, the resistance and the determination to resist has spread to every district, to every village, to every hamlet, to every house and to every Vietnamese heart.

This is very important to understand. Every man, woman and child in this country has a determination like a bright flame, buoying them, strengthening their determination to go forward, to fight for freedom and independence.

And what interests me so much as an American, is that this is so much like the essence of the American people. The one unifying quality I believe about the American people, the common denominator that we all share, is the love for freedom and democracy. The problem is that the definition of freedom and democracy has been distorted for us and we have to redefine what that means. But the Vietnamese who have been fighting for four thousand years know very well.

And as in Nam Dinh, for example, all the rubble and all of the destruction has not stopped them. It is fascinating to see. There are people still living there, there is still electricity in the city. The factory has been dispersed, but it is still working. The textiles are still being produced. Families are still producing food for a living. They are still going to the markets, and they are still ready to pick up a gun if necessary and defend their homes and their land.

POWS CALL FOR PEACE

July 20, 1972, broadcast, after Fonda met with seven American POWs in Hanoi: Navy Commander Walter Wilber, Lieutenant Colonel Edison Miller, Air Force Major James Padgett, Navy Lieutenant Commander David Wesley Hoffman, Air Force Captain Kenneth James Fraser, Air Force Captain William G. Byrns, and Air Force Pilot Edward Elias.

This is Jane Fonda speaking from Hanoi. Yesterday evening, July 19, I had the opportunity of meeting seven U.S. pilots. Some of them were shot down as long ago as 1968 and some of them had been shot down very recently. They are all in good health. We had a very long talk, a very open and casual talk. We exchanged ideas freely. They asked me to bring back to the American people their sense of disgust of the war and their shame for what they have been asked to do.

They told me that the pilots believe they are bombing military targets. They told me that the pilots are told that they are bombing to free their buddies down below, but of course, we know that every bomb that falls on North Vietnam endangers the lives of the American prisoners.

They asked me to bring messages back home to their loved ones and friends, telling them to please be as actively involved in the peace movement as possible, to renew their efforts to end the war.

One of the men who has been in the service for many, many years has written a book about Vietnamese history, and I thought this was very moving, that during the time he's been here, and the time that he has had to reflect on what he has been through and what he has done to this country, his thoughts have turned to this country, the history of struggle and the people that live here.

They all assured me that they have been well cared for. They listen to the radio, they receive letters. They are in good health. They asked about news from home.

I think we all shared during the time that I spent with them a sense of deep sadness that a situation like this has to exist, and I certainly felt from them a very sincere desire to explain to the American people that this war is a terrible crime and that it must be stopped, and that Richard Nixon is doing nothing except escalating it while preaching peace, endangering their lives while saying he cares about the prisoners.

And I think one of the things that touched me the most was that one of the pilots said to me that he was reading a book called *The Draft* written by the American Friends Service Committee and that in reading this book he had understood a lot about what had happened to him as a human being in his sixteen years of military service. He said that during those sixteen years, he had stopped relating to civilian life, he had forgotten that there was anything else besides the military and he said in realizing what had happened to him, he was very afraid that this was happening to many other people.

I was very encouraged by my meeting with the pilots because I feel that the studying and the reading that they have been doing during their time here has taught them a great deal in putting the pieces of their lives back together again in a better way, hopefully, and I am sure that when they go home, they will go home better citizens than when they left.

"I DIDN'T THINK OF THAT"

July 24, 1972, broadcast.

This is Jane Fonda in Hanoi. Yesterday, I'm told that the record for B-52 bombing raids in Vietnam was set. United Press International reported that in "Operation Linebacker" against North Vietnam in the first ninety-nine days of the renewed air war in Vietnam, U.S. bombers flew more than 20,300 raids. In each of these raids, an average of two tons of bombs were dropped on the country.

Now, we know that B-52s are strategic bombers. These are planes that were built, invented, in the event that a large country with its own air force and heavy arsenal of military weapons, like Russia, would need to be attacked. To use B-52s against the civilian population is like trying to kill a butterfly with a machine gun. It's barbaric.

I am assuming that because you are so far away from the land here, because you are on the ships, or because you are in Thailand, or because you are so high up in the sky that you can hardly see what it is you're bombing, that you don't really realize what the effect of these bombs is.

The other day, someone told me about one of the pilots who was recently shot down near Hanoi. As he was driven across the river, being rescued by the people, he was shown a bridge and the people said, "That bridge was bombed recently." And he said, "Well, my parents are rich. We can buy you a new bridge, we can afford to build you a new bridge after the war." And the people said to him in Vietnamese and it was then translated by the interpreter, they said, "But can your parents replace our children, our mothers, our wives who have been killed by your bombs?" And the soldier hung his head and he said, "I didn't think of that."

I've heard this from several pilots: "I didn't think of that." I think that we have to start thinking about it. I think we have to start thinking about the incendiary bombs that are being dropped. These bombs asphyxiate people to death, people who are in the shelters. Now, who goes into the shelters? The women, the old people and the children. They're suffocating to death. They're being burned beyond imagination and I think that we have to think about that.

What are you being told by your commanders? Are you being told that you're bombing to help the people? To save the country for democracy? What kind of democracy? Fifty thousand American lives have been lost here for a one-man election. Is that a democracy? What kind of democracy is it when just after the last one-man election the Thieu regime in the south passed new economic reforms which were planned and set up by the United States?

And what, in fact, do these reforms do? They benefit the U.S. businessman. They give him tax exemptions to make the most incredible kinds of profits in South Vietnam. They will not have to pay taxes on the fortunes they are making off the riches in South Vietnam.

And this country is a rich country—the soil is rich, the tin, the tungsten, the rubber, the lumber. Eisenhower knew it well, that is why he said it was necessary for us to finance 85 percent of the

French-Indochina war against the Vietnamese people. The people in the Pentagon knew it. The Mekong Delta is called one of the riches pieces of real estate in Asia.

But what does this have to do with you? What does this have to do with the masses of people in America? It is not in our interest. In fact, it is quite the contrary. You knew that there is rising unemployment in the United States. There is, for the first time since 1893, a trade deficit, an imbalance of payments, inflation.

In fact, the war is falling on the backs of the working people of America. What are our corporate bosses doing? They are going into countries like Vietnam—or trying to—they're going into the Philippines, into Brazil, into Okinawa, into other what we call underdeveloped countries around the world and they're setting up factories which make component parts. One part will be made in the Philippines, another part will be made in Vietnam, another part will be made in Brazil. They would be assembled in Mexico and they'll be sold on the American market at American prices. But the American worker will not be given a job. Why are the bosses going elsewhere and why are they trying to go to Vietnam? Because the workers are paid from 40 to 90 percent less than the workers in the United States.

When you're on the ground in South Vietnam, you see the Esso sign and the Shell signs and the Coca-Cola signs and the Hondas and the TV sets. And is it for that you're fighting? Is that worth risking your life for? Is that worth killing innocent people for? I think not. And in fact, what is the war doing? The war is only making the people of Vietnam understand who their enemy really is. . . .

So I think that maybe American people have to begin to see clearly who is fighting who and for what. Should we be fighting on the side of the people who are murdering innocent people? Should we be trying to defend a government in Saigon which is putting in jail tens of thousands of people into tiger cages, beating them, torturing them? I have met some of these victims and it is a horrible thing to see.

And I don't think, as Americans, we who come from a country that was founded on freedom, independence, and democracy, that we should be risking our lives or fighting to defend that kind of government.

TRAITORS AND PATRIOTS

At this press conference in New York, Fonda showed the film that she had brought back from Hanoi. The sound (packed separately from the film) was reportedly held up in French customs in Paris, but it was never returned to her. The film itself would disappear shortly after she screened it at this press conference. The film showed her interview with the seven American POWs in Hanoi and extensive bombing damage, including bomb craters on dikes.

QUESTION: Most Americans think that you are brainwashed, Miss Fonda. I'm sure you have seen the emotional reaction to your trip. You've been called a traitor, Hanoi Rose, how do you answer them?

FONDA: I think that we always have to define what is a traitor and what is being a patriot. I cried every day that I was in Vietnam, but I never cried for the Vietnamese. I cried for the Americans. The bombs are falling on Vietnam but it is an American tragedy. And it will take the American people many, many years to wipe out the blight of this war and particularly, the barbaric crimes of the Richard Nixon administration which are escalating daily. I believe that the people in this country who are speaking out against the war are the patriots. I believe one day we are going to take our

CIA-prepared transcript of press conference, Drake Hotel, New York City, July 28, 1972.

history back, we will take the textbooks back, we will rewrite the textbooks so they will tell that truth about this country and the people who will be the patriots will be people who are fighting for the principles upon which this country was founded: equality, freedom and independence. What is the most disturbing thing is that the Vietnamese people are fighting for the exact same thing that the Americans fought the British for. And the fact that our country has been so turned around by people who are not patriots but murderers and that this is being done in the name of the American people—the slaughter of people who are fighting for their freedom—is something that every one of us should abhor. Everyone of us should speak out against it if we are true Americans.

Q: What will you do with the film when it is edited and the sound is put back into it? Would you be dispensing it to various places, to colleges?

FONDA: It will be seen and distributed to as many people as possible.

Q. [Tape unclear]

FONDA: I asked to see an antiaircraft gun and I was taken there, needless to say, when there were no American planes around because they were afraid that I would be bombed. I went there because I wanted to see who the men are who are firing these guns, what do they have to say for themselves, what do they find? I found a group of young men, they looked, as most Vietnamese do, a lot younger than they may be, they looked about seventeen, I think they were probably twenty-two or twenty-three. They sang me a song and they showed me the gun and I looked at the gun and a lot of people have misunderstood that. I applauded the singing and what they were singing. They were singing praises to the blue skies of Hanoi and hoping the war would end so there wouldn't have to be any more silver planes in the blue skies of Hanoi.

Q. Do you think that the American people would prefer the

statements of a woman who is primarily known as an actress as opposed to the president of the United States?

FONDA: There are many tens of thousands of people who are speaking out against the war, including members of the Johnson administration, including soldiers who fought there, including former military advisors. The My Lai massacre—look at the denials that came down about that until finally it was proven. Look at the denials about the bombing of the civilian targets until finally they couldn't deny it anymore. What was the big lesson of the Pentagon Papers? That a series of American administrations had seen the Americans as an obstacle to be gotten around so they could continue to carry out their schemes and, as far as I'm concerned, their murders, and I think that [it's] time that people shouldn't just believe but start thinking for themselves. . . .

I'm an American woman, I went as an American citizen and I saw with my own eyes. I am not the beginning or the end of this question, you know. There are too many other people who are saying the same things. We have evidence of the lies of this government and so we should, all of us, no matter how hard it is, let go of the American necessity to believe that "if he's in the White House, he's gotta be a saint." There's enough evidence now to prove that it is quite the contrary.

LIVING UP TO
OUR COUNTRY'S IDEALS

QUESTION: A lot of people have been saying that your trip to North Vietnam was a betrayal of this country. What is your reply?

FONDA: Have you read *Bury My Heart at Wounded Knee*? It's the Pentagon Papers of the wars against the American Indians. It chronicles the massacres that took place. And of course it didn't show Custer as a hero: it paints a picture of those massacres and that genocide in a way that we're not usually taught in school. I think we would all agree that there would have been nothing too extreme that could have been done at that time to stop the killing and the destruction of those Indian tribes. I think that twenty years from now . . . Eighty years from now, one hundred years from now, looking back on Vietnam, we will understand that there is nothing too extreme to stop the war. I think that we have a chance right now to end the war. . . . So I am saying here what I said in Hanoi: I think that anyone here, if they had seen what I saw, would have done the same thing. I think that the people who are betraying the democratic ideals upon which this country was founded are the people who are prolonging the war.

Q: Why has the peace movement been so dormant during the bombing?

Philadelphia (Sunday) Bulletin, October 1, 1972.

FONDA: Nixon knew the first month he was in office, from a secret memorandum which was recently published by Jack Anderson that, at the minimum, to pacify South Vietnam it would take
8.3 years and at the maximum it would take 13.4 years. In other
words, he knew that he would never maintain control over South
Vietnam as a neo-colony during his four years in office or his first
four years. And that's why the Vietnamization Program, a method
to pacify the American people to make us think that the war is
over—withdrawing ground troops, reducing American casualties.
What he doesn't tell us is that the air war is escalating, that there are
more planes, more ships, more aircraft carriers used than ever before.

There are not so many boxes coming home with dead American bodies in them. And Nixon has a very cynical attitude towards
the American people, assuming that we won't care that more
Asians are dying. That, as long as our cost in terms of lives is reduced, we can be quieted. It's a very confusing thing for most people. He is making it look, on the one hand, that the war is ending;
on the other hand, he's telling us that a civil war is taking place in
Vietnam and that there are two countries there, North Vietnam
and South Vietnam, that are fighting each other and that we're
backing one side against the North Vietnamese invasion. We're
being lied to: our minds are being tampered with. So if the peace
movement seems to be going dormant, it's because people are
confused.

Q: You must be high on the government's list of undesirable
people. Have you had experience of harassment?

FONDA: My bank account statements have been taken illegally.
The FBI went to the bank and they took it, with coercion. And I
have the documents—they were given to me by Jack Anderson.
They took all my bank account statements to see who I'm con-
tributing money to.

Q: Because of your views on the war, is there any pressure from the motion picture industry affecting your career?

FONDA: No. As long as they can make a buck off me, they'll hire me.

Q: How does your stature as an actress affect your ability to work in the peace movement? Has your role as a glamour girl opened doors for you in the peace movement?

FONDA: It has made it more difficult in the sense that our society tends to have people put into categories and, especially if anyone has ever been categorized as a glamour girl, it's very difficult to get out of that, given the chauvinism in this country, given sexual stereotypes. So I always have to overcome that, and I always have to explain myself a great deal more than people—men, say—people who have not been performers. But I think that's becoming less and less a problem.

Q: After the war is ended, what does the future hold for you? Will you resume your acting career?

FONDA: I'm an actress and I'm continuing my acting career. I have not given it up, except that I have suspended it between now and November, because I think that this is really a unique time. And we will continue the Indochina Peace Campaign until the war ends. This is just a very escalated push. Yes, I will be making films.

Q: Has it opened doors for you?

FONDA: Oh, I think a lot of people come to hear me because I'm an actress. Certainly. I don't care. What I care about is what they leave with.

Q: Would you welcome a commission of inquiry into your activities?

FONDA: I wouldn't welcome it. I think it would be a waste of time and American tax dollars. There are more important things to do. But if ever that happens, I would certainly go. I would go and I would talk and I would say what I have. I wish that they would publish, for example, my broadcasts—these broadcasts that they've been poring over to find if there's any crime that I've committed. I wish the American people could see what I have said. I wish that I could show my films to people in Congress.

Q: Since you are an activist, if the war were not an issue—if the war were over—what would you be speaking out against next?

FONDA: Lies. Lies. I have to go back to the McCarthy era. I know what that did to people in this country. I saw it, I lived through it, I felt it, I know what it did to me. I know what it did to my school friends and my teachers. I know who Nixon is. I deeply resent the fact that we're being lied to, that our government is corrupt, that the burden of all the policies of the Nixon administration are falling on the working people of America. I would talk about it because I think that getting this off our backs, opening our minds up, getting this kind of person and these kinds of policies out of this country—I don't mean out of America, I mean out of our capital, out of office—is what is going to save us. If we don't, it's going to be at the loss of our souls. It's going to be at the loss of democracy in this country. We'll have a structure left. We'll have free elections. But what will it mean? The people we're electing won't be sensitive to our needs and desire, will supersede our representatives and will lie to us, will deceive us.

Q: Despite everything you feel, do you have faith in the future of this country and do you think there are some good things about it?

FONDA: Yes, I really do. And you know what? This is going to sound bizarre, but the place where I gained the most confidence in the United States was in Vietnam, from the Vietnamese people. One of the committees that invited me is called the Committee of Solidarity with the American People. They educate the people of Vietnam—and they're essentially peasants—about who we are. They send people into the countryside—to the areas that are most heavily bombed—to talk to the people about the peace movement in America, about Jefferson, Abraham Lincoln, Thomas Paine—to educate them about our history.

They said to me that it's very important that our people not hate. It's very important that they understand who the American people are—that there is a difference between the American people and the American government.

The Vietnamese believe, and they gave me great optimism, that we will live up to the democratic ideals upon which this country was founded. They have an absolute fundamental belief in that. And they believe that by resisting and defeating the forces that are betraying those ideals, then they are helping us. They see themselves linked very closely with the people in this country, and how tragic it is that people in this country don't know anything about the Vietnamese.

A VIETNAM JOURNAL: BIRTH OF A NATION

Tom Hayden, myself and our nine-month-old son Troy arrived April 1st in Hanoi. It was my second visit and Tom's fourth, but it would be the longest stay for either of us. It was prime time for an extended visit, the country was once again rebuilding in the wake of war and the south was facing the prospect of an interminable "new war" which had begun almost simultaneously with the much-heralded cease-fire. So we left Troy in good hands in Hanoi and proceeded on a two-week journey south with director/ cinematographer Haskell Wexler and a cameraman and a sound man from the Democratic Republic of Vietnam. The film is currently being edited and is due to be finished in the fall. It will be distributed through the Santa Monica–based Indochina Peace Campaign. What follows is a series of recollections—in journal form—of what I saw, heard and felt as the entourage made its way from Hanoi to the liberated zone of Quang Tri Province.

Even though the war continues in the South, the bombing has stopped over the North—who knows for how long—and so the people of the North have thrown themselves into reconstruction. Housing, schools, transportation routes, health facilities are the immediate necessities being rebuilt. . . . Almost everything seems to

"A Vietnam Journal: Birth of a Nation," *Rolling Stone,* July 4, 1974.

be done by hand, although there are a few trucks and cranes around. . . . To appreciate fully the spirit and resolve with which the Vietnamese seem to be facing the task of reconstruction, one has to bear in mind the extent of the destruction. Any visitor will quickly notice that virtually all large structures and many small ones, every bridge, every roadway, especially outside of Hanoi, have been bombed. The debate over whether the Pentagon "intended" to target more than "military" structures, however historians decide it, will not change the fact that nearly everything was bombed. The catalogue of reconstruction needs is total.

This is the *third time* these same people have begun rebuilding their country in thirty years. After a ten-year war against the French who were defeated in 1954, we were told there remained only 100 kilometers of railroad and one narrow highway. In the next ten years they began to build a new Vietnam in the North. Then in 1965, Johnson began the air war and all this was wiped out. Following the bombing halt in 1969, they once again set about rebuilding, but in 1972, Nixon resumed the bombing and this time nothing was spared. All the industrial centers, dams, dikes, state farms were hit. Every provincial hospital in the North was bombed at least once as well as crowded residential centers, schools, pagodas, cathedrals. With the exception of the center of Hanoi, which was avoided for diplomatic reasons, every other city in the North has to be rebuilt. . . .

Article 21 of the peace agreement commits the United States to help in reconstruction but the Nixon administration has refused and is even blocking U.S. funds to a UNICEF program which would aid the children in North Vietnam. American people, however, have raised over a million dollars in the past year and a half, much of it in nickels and dimes, for medical aid to Indochina. This organization is committed to rebuilding the ear, nose, and throat wing of the Bach Mai hospital, of particular need since so many children and old people have been deafened by the concussion of the bombs. We were told that preliminary shipments of equipment have already arrived.

Tom and I had visited Bach Mai hospital previous to the 1972 Christmas terror bombing. I remembered many of the women doctors I had met. I see their strong faces every time we show our slides of "Women in Vietnam." When I asked to meet them again, I was told most of them were killed in the bombing, trying to get the patients out. The building where they were killed is a pile of rubble and there is a small monument in honor of them and the others who failed to escape . . .

We visited a bicycle factory in Thanh Hoa City where almost 200 workers, 80 of whom are women, turn out 400 bicycle frames a month, mostly from scrap metal of downed U.S. aircraft and bomb casings. The debris is melted down and hammered into spokes and frames. The factory director proudly showed us his own bike, part of which was made from the debris of the Johnson bombing and part from Nixon's bombing. In an annex, the scrap metal is melted down into pots and pans. Elsewhere, U.S. bombers are resurrected as rings, combs, vases and statuettes. Bomb casings become flower pots, the plastic-covered wire electronic barrier across the DMZ has now been fashioned into colorful purses sold in the marketplaces of Quang Tri. A miniature version of what a new village in Quang Tri will look like is made from unexploded shells. . . .

In Dong Ha we met with a group of artists, filmmakers and singers from a "Liberation Song and Dance Ensemble." I was introduced as "Jane who was Barbarella and now is dedicated to peace." It often seems to me that one of the qualities the Vietnamese hold most precious is people's ability to change. The change is what's of greatest importance, not what one used to be. At home I was more acceptable as Barbarella and the first antiwar speeches I ever gave were billed as "come and hear Barbarella speak!" Change is threatening. I lived a long time with all the trappings and mind-set of an

alienated culture. In fact, as an actress without a social consciousness, I was a promoter of that culture. Now, I not only have to deal
with exorcizing its effects on me but I have to consider what it
means that this same culture is being exported to other cultures.
(We found a translation of the hardcover comic book *Barbarella* on
sale in a hotel in Bangladesh while newspapers spoke of the threat
of famine).

I have seen "Yankee go home" written on walls in quite a few
countries. Yet here in Vietnam, even in 1972, I never heard or saw
any anti-American slogans. They would point to bomb craters and
say accusingly, "Johnson" or "Nixon," depending on how fresh the
craters were, but never, "Yankee." I marveled at this lack of hostility
toward Americans until I began to discover that there has been a
monumental effort on all levels to help Vietnamese people understand who we are, our history and culture.

The Committee of Solidarity is mainly responsible for this
work. American history has been translated into Vietnamese so
they knew about Thomas Paine and Lincoln as well as racism and
genocide. Films of the antiwar movement were shown by mobile
film units which travel from village to village. They sing progressive American songs they learned from Joan Baez and Pete Seeger
or by listening to western radio. Steinbeck and Hemingway are
popular and an American journalist found a copy of *Huckleberry
Finn* on the body of a young schoolboy who'd been killed by a
bomb.

One afternoon in 1972 I sat on a lawn at an eleventh-century
university in Hanoi called the Temple of Literature, watching a
play. I remember the sound of an air-raid alert in the distance as I
watched a performance of Arthur Miller's *All My Sons*. It tells of an
American factory owner during World War II whose plant makes
cylinders for bombers. He discovers that the cylinders are faulty
but he doesn't say anything for fear of losing his government contract and all his money and as a result planes crash, and men are

killed, including one of his own sons. A remaining son finds out what his father has done and condemns him for his crime of silence, saying that there is no excuse for not living up to our social responsibility; not money, comfort, nor family loyalty. The play was presented by a troupe of professional actors who traveled in the countryside to perform the play for peasants whose homes had been destroyed in order to help the peasants understand the contradictions in our society so that they would not hate us. It has been performed there nearly one hundred times.

We saw the play again in April 1974, this time in a 700-seat theater where Haskell filmed the final act and I watched the audience carefully. They were rapt and cheered such lines as the doctor saying, "Most of my clients are mentally ill. Money . . . money . . . money. I wish I could live long enough to see money lose its importance." We interviewed the actors afterward and I asked them why they had chosen this play. "People can see it and can understand better what Americans are like," one of them told us. "The son is a good person. So they see that in America there aren't just capitalists but good people. Our people have learned who the real enemy is. We make the distinction between the American people and the American government."

The poet Nguyen Dinh Tri put it this way: "History has led our two people to encounter each other in tragic circumstances. The U.S. war of aggression has shown what is worst and what is best in your country. For us, the Vietnamese, during the bombing it was criminal. From distinguished and respected leaders they [the U.S. government] fell to the ranks of criminals. Not only criminals, but political crooks. But on the other hand, the war caused to well up in America what is most fine and noble. The sense of responsibility to us and to yourselves. Particularly in the beginning when protestors were still very isolated. Then one had to really believe in the justice of your cause." . . .

It's a two-and-a-half-day jeep ride from Hanoi to the DMZ

[demilitarized zone] down Highway One. The highway is, in fact, barely a road, hardly wide enough for trucks to pass and paved only two-thirds of the way. Sometimes we'd have to lurch through rocky riverbeds to avoid a bomb crater or a partially repaired bridge, but the very fact that we were able to make the trip was, in itself, a testament to the Vietnamese victory against the bombs. . . .

The going was rough. Not just the heat and dust, but the view from the jeep was a sobering one and we had a lot of time to think about the meaning of this trip. If technological power was the determining factor, Vietnam would long ago have become an American satellite. How many wars will it take us to learn that the defense budget can be increased and missile systems perfected till all our cities rot, but as long as the United States pits itself against the wishes of people who want to be their own masters and who are united in defending that principle, then the U.S. will fail.

Who would have believed years ago, before the new reality of "people's war" impressed itself on our consciousness, that the U.S. could fail against a country of peasants, withdraw planes, ships, and men short of victory, and negotiate an agreement leaving "enemy" forces strong and intact? It has never happened to us before but then computers don't work in combating a "people's war," for it is humans who program the computers and what can they who have themselves been programmed know? How could they envision teams of young school girls devising ways to defuse time bombs that have been dropped at night, soldiers walking for months with dismantled tank parts on their backs, these soldiers being fed and sheltered by the peasants who never give away their secret? Would they imagine that a team of women, working at night, can fill a bomb crater with their hands in a few days to keep the traffic going, or that the men at the boat landing would sink their ferry during the day to hide it from the planes and pump it out every night so it could be used?

And here we were, going down Highway One, watching the

train pass by crammed with people, seeing the men and women re-pairing the road, passing rocks and chunks of earth down a human chain and leveling it out, the denuded landscape planted with young saplings, the forests of the future. A nation being rebuilt, by hand.

The further south we got, the rougher the road became, the closer together the bomb craters, the more barren the land. "It's been a long year, you should have seen it before," we were told.

At the end of the second day, we arrived in the district of Vinh Linh which is in the part of Quang Tri Province situated just north of the DMZ. Not only is Quang Tri divided, but even the village of Vinh Linh is half in the North, half in the South.

I had read about it, and seen filmmaker Jeris Ivan's superb documentary, *The 17th Parallel,* shot before Vinh Linh was razed. Ten tons of bombs per person were dropped on this district which had once been very fertile with rich vegetation and nice two-story houses. Now all that remains are the pillars of the water reservoir.

Much has been rebuilt in the past year but still we could see the vast spaces where the earth looks like death. Dead earth. Our inter-preter explained that the bombing plows up the earth and gives the topsoil this strange look. We walked around two craters made by 500-pound bombs dropped by B-52s to watch four shiny new Russian tractors leveling the land, preparing for the fall harvest. A woman worker told us that during the war they continued work-ing and "when they attacked we went into the tunnels. When they left we went back to work. This way, despite the destruction, we al-ways had enough to eat. And we would sing. Our motto was 'Let our singing drown out the sound of the bombs'!"

We asked to visit these tunnels she spoke of. Tom and I had heard about the underground "city" of Vinh Linh, labyrinths going deep into the ground with large meeting halls, water wells, classrooms, delivery rooms. Seventy thousand people had been forced to live in them by the bombing.

We descended, stooping with lanterns, into the long, black, dark, earthen tunnels, passing tiny four-by-eight cubicles which jutted off the main passages at regular intervals. Each one "housed" a family. One was the "delivery room" where seventeen children were born. Because of prolonged lack of oxygen and sunlight in the tunnels, there have been problems of skin diseases, tuberculosis and rheumatism, particularly with the children and old people.

After ten minutes (we hadn't even reached the larger meeting halls) all I wanted was to get out. Tom and I realized we didn't know anyone we thought could survive this underground life. Yet Mr. Diet, a seventy-year-old fisherman we later interviewed, told us he had spent much of three years here "because we never knew when the bombs would come. When they stopped, we would go out to sea and fish and then go back to the tunnels. The bombs would fall near the boat and the waves would turn the boat over. Sometimes the boat was hit and once I had to swim one kilometer to shore." Mr. Diet told us that his home had been bombed and shelled by the 7th Fleet. He and his friends had rebuilt it six times.

The Ben Hai River marks the 17th parallel, or the middle of what was once the DMZ. We arrived on a peaceful Sunday morning after a half-hour's drive from Vinh Linh. The large red and gold flag of the Provisional Revolutionary Government (PRG) waved across the river. The decade of American strategy that had tried to create a barricade was past, and now peasants, fisherman, water buffalo and some trucks came and went across the narrow pontoon bridge. "They could destroy the metal bridge, but not the bridge in our hearts," we were told by an officer who had been at the bridge since 1955.

We waited at the bridge for the return of our passports and visas. The PRG has its own procedures. I gazed back at the river. The Ben Hai is not very wide. A fisherman could cast across it with a good breeze at his back. Villages dot its banks, some are divided by the river. Members of the same family often live on either bank, yet after 1954, visitors from the North would be considered invaders. We received our documents and walked across the bridge to the liberated zone of Quang Tri. . . .

The province of Quang Tri was the most heavily bombed area of South Vietnam. It was an area of strategic importance for many reasons, including the invasion of Laos in 1971 and the site of battles for Camp Carroll, Highway Nine and Khe Sanh. It was also the first area to be liberated in the 1972 offensive when U.S./Saigon forces retreated and abandoned multimillion-dollar bases such as Ai-Tu, Khe Sanh and Cua Viet Port. Having failed to control the territory, the United States tried wiping it off the map with round-the-clock B-52 carpet bombings, napalm attacks, defoliation agents and chemical gases.

When the U.S. forces pulled out, they left behind untold numbers of unexploded mines, more frightening perhaps than bombs because they are unseen. There is no droning of an aircraft, no warning air alert, only a beckoning field that must be cultivated if there is to be a full harvest. Two or three times a day, the light tread of a rubber sandal brings crippling wounds or death.

Just to construct the guest quarters we stayed in, which are approximately the size of a square city block, 400 mines had to be detonated. We were told that in the year following the signing of the peace agreement, 300 people and 1,000 buffalo have been killed in Quang Tri by the mines. The mines are difficult to detect because of the massive amounts of scrap metal just beneath the soil. Controlled burning of mine-laden areas has been only minimally effective.

The problem is not limited to Quang Tri. The Study Mission of the Kennedy subcommittee on refugees reports that throughout Indochina, people face "some 300,000,000 to 600,000,000 pounds of explosives that may blow up in their fields and forests for years to come."

One morning we visited the provincial hospital of Quang Tri.

During the carpet bombing, the hospital had been evacuated to the jungle. Now it is rebuilt on the rubble with 150 beds, 15 doctors and 35 nurses. . . . Suddenly we saw two men running with a stretcher toward the hospital. It was wet with blood and as it passed I saw a young man's face, already ashen and gasping for air. He died a minute or so later. Bled to death. His name was Le Van Ba; he was twenty-six years old. A few minutes later, a second stretcher was rushed in with the body covered. Bui The Doanh had died on the way to the hospital. Altogether, four people had been hit by a mine two kilometers away, near the port of Cua Viet where we had been the day before.

The only official statement by U.S. sources about unexploded mines and bombs came in response to a refugee subcommittee request in August 1973, "The clearing of ordnance . . . has so far not been a major problem," U.S.A.I.D. replied. The Study Mission report quoted earlier concludes, "To date, neither the Pentagon nor the U.S.A.I.D Mission seems to have accepted the thought that there may be some degree of U.S. responsibility, even indirectly, in this area" . . .

Further south on Highway One is the Ai-Tu base. Ai-Tu means "Love the Children." The base covered twelve square kilometers. It was the largest logistics base and included 300 buildings, an airport for helicopters and transport planes, command headquarters, repair, telecommunication and radio centers and warehouses.

On April 27, 1972, the PRG encircled the base and three days later took control. What remains after the bombing is rusting, twisted steel strips of runway as far as we could see, thousands of oil drums scattered on the ground, tangled barbed wire and many portable steel bunkers being used by the peasants who have returned to claim their land. An old man who has built a little shack at the edge of the runway sat in the shade of his squash vine and said to us, "They didn't want to leave. But I saw them defeated."

At the western end of Ai-Tu is a village of 3,000 people who had been rounded up into four camps in the early 1960s by American GIs. "Our sufferings became especially horrible when the special war began," the village head explained. "The people were rounded up into strategic hamlets. In September 1967, when the U.S. built the base, they used bulldozers to raze 1,800 graves and about 600 houses and gardens. Thousands of buffalo and oxen died. Where we are now used to be a hamlet. Even before building the base, the U.S. carried out the "Three Alls": kill all, burn all, destroy all. A typical case was July 10, 1967, when GIs killed twelve people, including three old people, and crippled one girl. After they rounded us up, we were not allowed to go out and do farming except at certain hours. There was starvation in the camp. We had to hire ourselves to the Americans. The women worked as servants and prostitutes and were often raped. Once twelve GIs raped one woman. She had severe hemorrhages."

Later, we filmed an interview with a village elder, a man in his late seventies.

"I was born here and so were my ancestors. I have four children, three sons and one daughter. The oldest son was killed by the French in 1944. My other children are in the liberated zones in other provinces, so only my wife and myself are here. I joined the anti-French resistance at 30 and was chairman of the local front. The French received aid from the U.S. The Japanese were here, too. After they were defeated, it was the French who came back, and then the Americans taking over from the French. Since 1945, I have been able to live in peace only a few months, then there was the war with the French. Then after that we had peace for a short while but then Ngo Dinh Diem took power with the help of the U.S. and we had no more peace.

"In 1959 I was arrested for a second time and I underwent torture. I was tied to a bench and both legs and arms were tied and they poured soapy water into my nose and mouth. I was also beaten, and I still have pains. They said we were a communist family because my sons fought in the resistance."

We asked him if he thought he would ever see a peaceful and reunited Vietnam.

"Formerly, I so wanted to see peace that I said I only wanted to live long enough to see peace restored to my village and then I would be willing to die in one month. But now that we have peace here in this village, I say I only want to live long enough to see reunification, and then I will be able to die."

As he spoke, we could see the remains of the Ai-Tu base, like a footprint of a dying giant. In the distance was the Saigon flag . . . the "new war," as futile as the old war and as horrible. Lives being wasted, bodies mutilated, fortunes taken from rotting ghettos at home. And I thought, as I had thought in 1972, that this war is an *American* tragedy. The Vietnamese, for all their suffering, know why they have fought and who their enemy is. They also know why they want to live. If we Americans can have the courage to look again at Vietnam and learn the lesson she has to offer, learning in the process who we are, then perhaps we, too, will find we have something to live for.

LOOKING BACK ON VIETNAM

Thanks to all of you for being here.

So, I have written a book called *My Life So Far*. This is what I've been doing most of the last five years. As I approached my sixtieth birthday, seven years ago, I realized that, assuming I live to be ninety, give or take, the curtain would soon be rising on my third act and it wasn't a dress rehearsal. This was it. The last act. Better get it right.

Third acts are important. They can pull all the random bits and pieces of the first two acts into a cohesive whole—or not. I knew that for my third act to be a good one, I needed to understand what the first two were all about. To know where you're going you have to know where you've been.

So, on my fifty-ninth birthday I decided to research my life, figure out what patterns were hidden there, what bridges of continuity spanned the canyons of change, discover what lessons the past held for me.

The process of doing this changed me in unexpected, wonderful ways and that's when I decided to write my book. I realized that if I could be brave enough to go deep and tell the truth, it would help other people because, although there's a lot that's different about me—I'm privileged, financially independent, successful and

Speech prepared for the National Press Club, Washington, D.C., April 14, 2005.

famous—my story contains much that is universal. I wrote to that universality. I wanted to write my life in such a way that the reader would constantly put the book down to reflect on their own life, their own relationships.

I had often wondered why, for ten years, I have focused my energy on trying to help girls understand the ways in which gender stereotypes handicap their ability to speak up, to give voice to their authentic selves and why so many are anorexic and bulimic. I have sought to understand what sexual abuse does to a girl (one out of four have been sexually abused) and find ways to help them heal. And I have paid close attention to the often destructive ways in which boys need to prove their manhood.

I realized while writing my book that I have done these things because these are my issues. These were my mother's issues. There are many themes that run through my book—fear of intimacy, loss of voice, forgiveness and healing. But tonight I want to focus on one part of my life: Vietnam. My book is not *about* Vietnam, it's about the totality of my journey up until now, but Vietnam is certainly the most controversial part of it. I wrote about this period honestly and in depth because I think that for many, the story of what brought me into the antiwar movement, why I went to Hanoi and what happened there can be part of a healing process. I hope so. It's time.

I want to talk about Vietnam because much is relevant to today. We are engaged once again in a divisive war and it's never too late to learn from the past.

The war had been raging for seven years when I became active in trying to end it.

The irony is that it was American GI resisters to the war who I met while I was living in Paris who forced me to face the realities of that war, and it was painful. Part of my identity had been that I was a citizen of a country that, in spite of its internal paradoxes, represented moral integrity, justice, and a desire for peace. I had always assumed that wherever our flag was flying, that was the side of the angels. I'd been "Miss Army Recruiter" in 1959.

But, thanks to American soldiers, I began to understand that the war in Vietnam was a different kind of war than the one my father had won a Bronze Star in, a war that pitted our men against a people fighting for national independence, a war that by its very nature produced atrocities—saturation bombing, free-fire zones, body counts. I felt betrayed as an American, not by the soldiers who fought there, but by the government leaders who lied to us and sent them there. And the depth of my sense of betrayal was in direct proportion to my previous depth of certainty about the ultimate rightness of any U.S. mission.

Why had I not paid more attention and taken action sooner? It wasn't that I was lazy or lacked curiosity. I think it had to do with giving up comfort—and I don't mean material comfort. I mean the comfort that ignorance provides. Once you connect with the painful truth of something, you then *own* the pain and must take responsibility for it through action. Of course, there are people who see and then choose to turn away, but then one becomes an accomplice. Bertolt Brecht once said, "He who doesn't know is an ignoramus. He who knows and keeps quiet is a scoundrel."

So in 1970, seven years after the war had begun, I returned home because I didn't want to be a scoundrel. I wanted to do something.

What I did was become a civilian supporter of the G.I. Movement, in my opinion, the most vibrant, important and unprecedented part of the antiwar movement. The *fact* that large numbers of servicemen actively opposed the Vietnam war has been written out of our history books. The revisionist view is that all soldiers were pro-war and all antiwar activists were anti-soldier. This was not the case, at least not by the time I joined the movement.

The *civilian* anti–Vietnam war movement was primarily white and middle-class, and the Nixon administration constantly labeled us elites, intellectuals, out of touch with the heartland. The GI movement, on the other hand, was made up of working-class kids, sons of farmers and hard hats who couldn't afford college deferments, as well as rural and urban poor, and of blacks and Latinos. It was harder for Nixon to dismiss them in the same way, which is why he and his administration went to such lengths to infiltrate, spy, and disrespectfully discredit them as being "*alleged* soldiers and veterans." Those young men always made it clear: they'd gone over out of patriotism, they came back and spoke out, out of patriotism.

It is heartening that today, there is a burgeoning GI and veteran's movement against the war in Iraq. On March 21, the second anniversary of the invasion of Iraq, 5,000 protestors gathered near Fort Bragg in Fayetteville, North Carolina, the largest such protest since the one I attended there in 1970. Speakers included servicemen belonging to Iraq Veterans Against the War, Military Families Speak Out, Veterans for Peace, and Gold Star Families for Peace, as well as parents of fallen soldiers.

This is as important today as it was thirty years ago. Opposing the war can't be made to look unpatriotic when soldiers and their families are speaking out. People are realizing today that we can oppose the war and support the troops.

It is true that the antiwar GIs represented a minority of our overall Vietnam-era troops, but there was a sizable enough minority of them that in 1971 the Army reported an almost 400 percent increase in AWOLs in five years; enough that military historian, retired Marine Corps Colonel Robert D. Heinl Jr. wrote in *Armed Forces Journal*: "By every conceivable indicator, our army that now remains in Vietnam is in a state approaching collapse, with individual units avoiding or having refused combat, murdering their officers and non-commissioned officers, drug-ridden, and dispirited where not near-mutinous . . ."

We mustn't condemn the Vietnam-era soldiers for the things cited by Heinl. Clearly, when you ask soldiers to fight and perhaps die in a dehumanizing war they no longer believe in, you should expect terrible consequences.

By the end of the 1960s, GIs had began to organize, not just around the growing antiwar sentiment within the military ranks, but in response to the undemocratic nature of the military itself. The young men believed that donning a uniform and defending their country didn't mean giving up their rights and their consciousness.

I know the military is important. We need a strong military. But the military isn't supposed to be dehumanizing and it hasn't always been so. It wasn't when my father was in the navy in World War II. Defensive wars against oppressive regimes do not require dehumanization. The problem was that in Vietnam, dehumanization was necessary because, rather than being a defensive war, it was a war of outside aggression (ours) against the desire of the majority of Vietnamese to be independent. I know this is a hard statement for many Americans to hear. "Come on," some of you may be thinking, "North Vietnam invaded South Vietnam." But Vietnam was and is one country that had been artificially divided by foreigners. We were lied to. Imagine if the British, back during our American Revolution, had created a boundary at our Mississippi River, labeling as "enemy" anyone who came across, whether to see family or to fight for reunification of their country.

I spent almost three years helping get the word out about what was happening to many GIs and how they were feeling. I was asked to represent the GI movement at many antiwar rallies. I helped open the GI Office here in D.C., which acted as an ombudsman for soldiers, a place where GIs could call or write, where acts of military injustice could be documented and where doctors and lawyers could verify their claims and get information about it to the House and Senate for investigation. It was staffed by Master Sergeant Donald Duncan, a much-decorated member of the Special Forces. Within months of its opening, we were receiving 500 letters a month.

I traveled to bases all over this country to listen to GIs who gathered in off-base GI coffeehouses. Together with a troupe of entertainers, I traveled to U.S. bases stateside and in Hawaii; Okinawa, Japan; and the Philippines with a show called Free the Army. All told, 60,000 servicemen and some women attended the shows.

At first, we assumed we'd be mainly performing for soldiers and sailors, but suddenly in the spring of 1971, the Air Force erupted with antiwar sentiment. You see, while President Nixon was trying to convince the American people that he was winding down the war—he called in Vietnamization: bringing our ground troops home and turning the war over to the Vietnamese—what he was really doing was escalating the war from the air.

Those of us who followed the war closely knew what was happening. So did members of the Air Force. Almost weekly, more planes were being shot down and more U.S. pilots were being captured. In response, the Air Force's desertion rate doubled; Travis Air Force Base in California, the primary embarkation point for flights to Vietnam, was in a state of siege for four days in May. In June, Sheppard Air Force Base in Texas saw a revolt. In August, Chanute Air Force Base in Illinois saw a violent uprising.

I spent a lot of time listening to members of the Air Force talk of their disillusionment with the war.

In the spring of 1972, reports began to come in from European scientists and diplomats that the dikes of the Red River Delta in North Vietnam were being targeted by U.S. planes. Those who had witnessed this felt it was deliberate.

We knew what this meant. By now, the Pentagon Papers were available and in them we read that, in 1966, Assistant Secretary of Defense John McNaughton, searching for some new means to bring Hanoi to its knees, had proposed destroying North Vietnam's dikes, which, he said, if handled right, would flood the rice fields and cause starvation. He estimated maybe a million. In 1972, Henry Kissinger estimated that, if the dikes collapsed, around 200,000 would starve.

To his credit, President Johnson had not acted upon this option. Now, six years later, Richard Nixon appeared to have given orders to target the dikes—whether to actually destroy them or to demonstrate the threat of destruction, no one knew.

The Red River Delta in North Vietnam, like Holland, is below sea level and the thousands of miles of hand-built, earthen dikes are what hold back the sea.

The Nixon administration was vehemently denying bombing the dikes except maybe by accident. But last fall, thanks to help provided by former Nixon White House counsel John Dean, I discovered in the National Archives heretofore unreleased White House tapes. Let me read some excerpts from a May 4, 1972, transcript of a conversation between President Nixon and H. R. Haldeman.

NIXON: We need to win the goddamned war . . . and . . . what that fella [?] said about taking out the goddamned dikes, all right, we'll take out the goddamned dikes. . . . If Henry's for that, I'm for it all the way.

H.R. HALDEMAN: I don't know if he's for the dikes.

NIXON: No, I don't think he's for the dikes, but I am.

[Later in same conversation]

NIXON: I agree with Connally about civilians too. I'm not going to worry about it.

We didn't know about these tapes back then, but we knew something bad was happening. The stability of these dikes becomes especially critical as monsoon season approaches. It was June. The Red River would begin to rise in July and August; the bombing showed no signs of letting up; and there was little press coverage of the impending disaster should the dikes be weakened and give way. Something drastic had to be done.

That's why I decided to go to North Vietnam. I wanted to expose the lies and bring back filmed evidence, if there was evidence (which there was), that the dikes were being bombed. Almost 300 Americans had gone to North Vietnam before me—scientists, Nobel Prize winners, activists, priests, diplomats, reporters, Vietnam veterans—over eighty had spoken over the radio there. I knew that my trip would be controversial, but I felt I had to go. And I'm glad I did. I returned in July after two weeks there. The bombing of the dikes stopped in August. If my trip and the footage I brought back played even a small role in that, it was worth it.

But I committed a terrible lapse of judgment on my last day there. I sat on an anti-aircraft gun. A group of soldiers had sung me a song, I had sung one back, everyone was laughing and clapping and someone asked me to sit down, pictures were taken by reporters and I didn't realize until a moment after I got up what the implication of that image would mean. The gun was inactive, there were no planes overhead, I simply wasn't thinking about what I was doing, only about what I was feeling—innocent of what the photo implies. Yet the photo exists, delivering its message, regardless of what I was really doing or feeling.

I had spent over two years working with GIs and Vietnam veterans and had spoken before hundreds of thousands of antiwar protesters telling them that our men in uniform *aren't* the enemy. I went to support GIs at their bases and overseas. In the years ahead, I would make *Coming Home* so that Americans could understand how the wounded were treated in veterans hospitals. Now, by mistake, I would appear in a photograph to be their enemy. I carry this heavy in my heart. I always will.

Quite a while after that, right-wing ideologues began to create a myth about me that is larger than life, certainly larger than me.

They need the myth to promote their own narrow, right-wing agenda and view of the war. This myth isn't about me, it's about them. It's a means to an end. I find it hard to understand the sheer anger that drives these attackers. They do a terrible disservice to our country and its people by burying the lessons we have to learn about the Vietnam war.

I have learned personal lessons from that: that what is in my heart isn't necessarily what will appear. I have also learned how critical it is today for citizens to be active, to stay involved, to search for the truth and to speak out no matter how the government tries to frighten us into silence.

Our government is fully capable of lying to us to prolong a war, even if it means losing American lives. I also learned that no matter what the personal costs, to remain quiet about it once you know, is a sin against humanity, a betrayal of the beliefs our country was founded on, and a travesty of moral values—Christian values.

There are still those who would have us believe that the United States could have won the war had we "gone all out," had we not been hampered by the antiwar movement. Of course. People had to be made to believe this so as to quell protest. Being antiwar must be made to appear anti-soldier so the administration can wage all-out, unimpeded war like in the good old days. But if Vietnam continues to be interpreted as a war which could have been won had we just prosecuted it differently, then we've learned nothing. The only way that the Vietnam tragedy won't happen again is to avoid wishful thinking and to understand it accurately.

But the real question isn't how we prosecuted the war, but whether the entire enterprise in Vietnam was wrong from the get-go. Thank God for the antiwar movement. Had it not been for the soldiers, the veterans and the civilians who opposed the war, it might have dragged on even longer.

For me, the overriding question about the war became why five administrations—Democratic and Republican—*knowing,* according to the Pentagon Papers, that we couldn't win militarily short of annihilation, *knowing* they would have to keep escalating to avoid losing—*why* would they choose to continue? Why postpone failure if it meant more loss of life? This is a question that is acutely relevant today—"Well, it may have been a mistake but now that we're there. . . ."

I will end with what I see as the answer and its implications: I believe that the unwillingness of president after president to cut their losses and withdraw had to do with the fear of being seen as unmanly, "soft." Back then it was "soft on Communism," today it's "soft on terrorism." Daniel Ellsberg, who has logged in a lot of hours studying United States policy in Vietnam, seems to agree. In an interview with *Salon* in November 2002, he said, "My best guess is that Lyndon Johnson psychologically did not want to be called weak on communism. As he put it to Doris Kearns, he said he would be called an 'unmanly man' if he got out of Vietnam, a weakling, an appeaser." Ellsberg went on, "Many Americans have died in the last fifty years, and maybe ten times as many Asians, because American politicians feared to be called unmanly."

In his book *War and Gender*, Joshua Goldstein, a professor of international relations at American University, writes: "As war is gendered masculine, so peace is gendered feminine. Thus the manhood of men who oppose war becomes vulnerable to shaming."

We know the labels hurled at men who oppose war and support diplomatic solutions: wimps, pussies, or girlie men. Beware of those who use words that relate pejoratively to the female when describing the "other side." For them, national omnipotence and their own potency are joined. They'd rather disappear from public life as Lyndon Johnson did than be blamed for premature evacuation. The most dangerous leaders are those (usually, but not always, men) who were bullied and shamed by their parents (usually, but not always, their fathers). Going to war rather than addressing social inequities will be their way of proving themselves qualified to

belong to the Manhood Club, which sees strength (often manifested as violence, homophobia) and hierarchy (manifested as
racism and misogyny) as their ticket in.

What a price is paid by those men and boys who eschew membership in the Manhood Club and choose instead to remain emotionally literate and empathetic. It's not easy being called those
names by our bullying leaders. We need to recognize, love and
salute the men who resist. We have to raise sons who resist.

This has all become so blatant during the last few years that it
seems like a parody. Look at the macho posturing in relation to the
Iraq war: "Bring, 'em on," "Are you man enough?" "I knew that
my God was bigger than his." The patriarchal "mine's bigger-
than-yours" drive for control has the entire world tilted in dangerous imbalance, damaging not only individual women, men and
children, but entire peoples. Gloria Steinem has written that "if we
are to stop producing leaders whose unexamined early lives are
then played out on a national and international stage" we need to
change patriarchal institutions.

I've thought a lot about this over the last five years, not only as it
relates to war but also to our personal relationships. I realized that
patriarchy is anathema to relationship because it depends on the
bifurcation of head and heart for its very existence. This toxic paradigm is so ingrained that we think it's just the way things are.

The opposite of patriarchy isn't matriarchy, it's democracy.
There's a fundamental contradiction, not just between patriarchy
and peace or between patriarchy and relationship, but between patriarchy and democracy. How can it be democracy when women,
who are a majority of the world's people, live in a system that discriminates against them and wants to keep them from having their
full human rights, and wages all-out backlash if they start to win
those rights? How can it be a democracy when leaders, to prove
their dominance and their nation's dominance, lie to their people
and send our youth to die?

Maybe at some earlier stage in human evolution, patriarchy was what was needed just for the species to survive. But today, the patriarchal paradigm is killing us and the earth. Surely the creator meant for there to be a balance between the masculine and feminine, the yin and the yang. Surely Jesus represented that divine balance.

So let's redefine masculinity. Let's define a *democratic manhood* whose virility is not dependent on dominance. Doing this, changing society to create real democracy, end the head/heart bifurcation and enable relationship, is a very political act—it means creating a social, cultural and psychic revolution.

So let's do it.

Part III

For Girls (and Boys)

GLOBAL EDUCATION FOR GIRLS AND WOMEN

Studying the lives and developmental issues of girls, I've done a lot of thinking about my own girlhood. I also have one biological daughter and two adopted daughters.

I want to start by telling a story about girls in a developing country because it's such a dramatic illustration of what happens when girls are empowered through education and work, and because I think that its lessons are true anywhere in the world.

Deep in the heart of Cairo, Egypt, at the bottom of a deep rock quarry, is an impoverished community of 17,000 Coptic Christians. These are the adults and children who collect the city's garbage. They haul garbage day and night in mule-drawn wagons or dilapidated trucks, from around the city to their community, and dump it into the center of their homes. Wet, soggy, putrefying, terrifying garbage, day after day, year after year.

They live in dark, primitive, door-less structures with dirt floors. Garbage piles sometimes reach six feet high. They cohabit with the garbage—it is their furniture, their couches and chairs. In the back of each home are pigs that eat the garbage. The pig excre-

"Jane Fonda Speaks on Global Education for Girls and Women," *Harvard Education Review,* July/August 2000.

ment is taken and dumped into a huge pit in the center of the community where it composts and then is sold as fertilizer.

Children crawl through the garbage. Older ones, mostly girls, sit on the dirt floors sorting through the garbage, removing anything that won't compost. During the day a few of the boys attend school, but no girls. There is no reason for parents to educate girls or invest in the education of their daughters. Girls are used as their mothers were before them—sorting garbage, taking care of their brothers and sisters, cooking the meals.

They are responsible in large part for the health of the family but they can't read prescriptions the doctors might give them and they are not accustomed to discussing things with doctors. When they enter puberty they are married, frequently earlier than the legal age of sixteen that Egyptian law permits. A girl may be married off to someone she doesn't choose, doesn't know, and who may be many, many years older than she.

Once married, a girl moves into her husband's house and goes to work for her mother-in-law. In other words, girls marry and leave home. Boys marry and bring a wife (read "servant") into his family's home. Better to invest in boys.

And so the crippling cycle of deeply ingrained gender bias is repeated generation after generation, driving high fertility rates and poor health, *until now.*

Six years ago, when I was in Cairo for the United Nations Conference on Population and Development, I asked to visit this community, to see a remarkable non-governmental project that I had heard about. I was driven into the community past the garbage-filled wagons, past the compost pit. When the car door opened, I was assailed by a stench thicker and more unbearable than anything I could have imagined. I had to breathe through my mouth so that I wouldn't get sick.

I forced myself out of the car, embarrassed to show the difficulty I was having. I couldn't believe that people lived their whole lives breathing this air. A Catholic num who developed and runs the project was there to meet me. First, she took me to a small school poised on the edge of the huge compost pit. There, I saw girls as well as boys, sitting at desks, studying. The nun told me that initially there was great resistance to sending the girls to school. To counter the resistance, the organizers had recently adopted a more holistic approach. I was led to a concrete building on the side of the hill to illustrate the point.

The rooms were filled with huge looms and paper-pressing machines. It was very clean. Girls were working everywhere, and they were clean, too. I was told the girls were taught to respect themselves by coming to work or going to school in a clean dress, usually their only one, with their hair short and their nails tidy. The girls were recycling paper fiber taken from the garbage, and making it into stationery and cards which they embroidered and sold. Other girls were at looms, weaving recycled bits of fabric into rugs. In another room, girls sat around a table, sorting pieces of colored fabric, leftovers donated by Cairo's textile shops. They were cutting them into squares, triangles, rectangles, applying what they had learned in school—math concepts that they had learned, to design symmetrical shapes, which they sewed into beautiful quilts.

And while they worked, they were being taught health concepts, including reproductive health, the dangers of early marriage and closely spaced births, and they learned about contraception. Some of them were also being trained to work as health outreach workers. Up to a sixth of the girls in the community are engaged in these income-generating programs, which pays them $17 a month. It's difficult for us in this country to imagine how $17 a month could be so transformative.

But understand the effect that it had. These girls had achieved a goal on their own, and they had been rewarded for it. Their sense of self was changed. A new world of possibilities had opened up. They could read, they could learn, they could earn, they could feel proud, they could just maybe break out of the cycle of servitude and despair.

Fathers and mothers began to view their girls in a new way. Now that the girls had developed income-generating skills, there was less resistance to educating them. Smart enough to read and to earn, they were becoming valuable assets to be encouraged rather than held back. Family health in the community began to improve, as girls learned to read and grew less timid about talking with doctors.

Another innovative part of the program was the creation of rewards to girls for delaying marriage. Delaying marriage gives them leverage and bargaining power with their families. Girls were offered 100 Egyptian pounds or $150 if they married after the age of eighteen, and if they freely chose their marriage.

Examples like this, and numerous others, are proof that in the developing world, if you change the lives of girls by educating them and give them the opportunity to become wage earners, it is a twofold gain. You expand human capital, while simultaneously improving reproductive health and slowing population growth. Giving girls the chance to delay marriage until a later age means they postpone the birth of the first child, and family size shrinks. Adolescent girls gain new status and identities beyond their traditional ones which define them narrowly as daughters, mothers, wives, sexual objects, and producers of male children. And for every additional year of schooling, a woman's income increases by up to 10 to 20 percent.

Typically, in some African countries, women with no education want seven children. Women with primary school education want a little more than three. And women with secondary education want only two. In Zimbabwe, Brazil, Mexico, and Peru, there is a four-child difference in desired family size between educated and non-educated women. Here is what U.S. Deputy Treasury Secretary Lawrence Summers said in a 1992 talk to the Economic Development Institute of the World Bank: "Investment in girls' education may well be the highest return investment available in the developing world." This is a view that is shared by a growing number of economists, including the World Bank itself.

For five years now I've been working in Georgia with an organization that I founded called the Georgia Campaign for Adolescent Pregnancy Prevention, or G-CAPP. The organization was conceived in Cairo at the same conference that brought me to the garbage collectors' community. Before then, I assumed that the solution to high-fertility rates was to provide more contraception. Now, obviously, more family planning is important, providing that it is of good quality, treats clients respectfully, offers contraceptive choices and is friendly to adolescents. This is important, but as I began to learn more, I realized that family planning is for people who want to limit their family size, who feel they have a right to protect themselves and the means to do so.

Unfortunately, far too few women do. The services that currently exist are not enough for poor women in both developed and developing countries and certainly not sufficient for adolescents who have so little control over their lives. I was beginning to learn that to understand and modify adolescent sexual and reproductive behavior, one must look beyond the traditional health-centered agenda. Sexual behavior, like all behavior, is determined by a complex web of social ties, based on factors such as race, class, gender, and ethnicity. It is these factors that determine the onset of sexual activity, family size, and the spacing of children.

Several years ago, I asked Dr. Michael Carrera, founder of one of this country's most successful adolescent pregnancy prevention programs, what is the single most important thing I could tell a mother who doesn't want her young daughter getting pregnant. And he answered, "Keep her in school and doing well." Making sure girls are educated is as important in this country as it is in the developing world.

Although education in the United States is required and acces-sible to boys and girls, at-risk youth too often dropout at early ages. School failure and dropping out are signs that a girl or boy has given up on himself or herself. Girls will then often turn to parent-hood as a way to obtain status and an adult identity within the family and the community. Rather than pregnancy being the cause of school dropout, as is too often believed, it is usually the other way around. In one recent study, a majority of dropouts had a baby more than nine months after they left school, a fact that clearly il-lustrates that the pregnancy could not have caused the dropout.

Teenage parents in this country tend not to be middle-class people who dropped out and became poor just because they had a baby. Well over half of all American women who give birth as teenagers come from profoundly poor families, and more than a fourth come from families who are slightly better off, but still struggling financially.

Altogether, more than 80 percent of teenage mothers are born poor and grow up in poor neighborhoods. Their girlhoods are often scarred by violence and disorder, including sexual abuse at the hands of a family member or friend. Chances are their mothers were themselves teenagers when they had them, and lacked the skills to prepare them for school or for life.

The schools they attend are too often run down and ill-equipped, with teachers having to struggle to discipline and moti-vate the students. And their life experiences rarely move them any closer to the American dream. Marion Wright Edelman, the founder and director of the Children's Defense Fund, says that "hope is the best contraceptive." Middle-class girls are more moti-vated to postpone sex, use contraception if they are sexually active, or get an abortion if they become pregnant, because they see a fu-ture for themselves that would be compromised by having a child too early.

Disadvantaged girls, on the other hand, see nothing to lose by early parenthood. In fact, for some adolescent girls who begin life at a disadvantage, motherhood can be a catalyst for turning their lives around. But for the majority of them, having a child makes it harder for them to take advantage of whatever opportunities and lucky breaks may come along. Public policy, to the extent that it exists at all in relation to adolescence, erroneously tends to assume that girls have considerable autonomy over their lives in general and their sex lives in particular. Another misconception is that male and female adolescents form a homogenous group with common needs and interests.

These misconceptions arise from a failure to recognize adolescent girls' disadvantages and the contrast in the experiences of boys and girls. In general, adolescence is a time of heightened vulnerability for girls, a time of silence, passivity, and devaluation, while for boys it is a time of increased power and social validity. Instead of demonizing young mothers, policymakers, in fact all of us, must recognize that their behavior is not always an expression of their own free will. In the area of sexuality, for instance, some studies show that 60 percent or more of mothers fifteen years and younger have been abused. The victim averages ten years old, the abuser averages twenty-seven years old, and most were adult male family members.

Childhood sexual abuse was the single biggest predictor of teenage pregnancy over the last forty years, according to a 1995 survey of 3,400 American adults, conducted by sociologists at the University of Chicago. When a girl has been sexually abused, she has also been brainwashed. Her sense of self, her sense of ownership of and control over her body, her capacity for self-efficacy is taken away. The question "Who am I?" is answered by "I am someone that exists to please others." This is what Oprah Winfrey, herself a victim of rape and violence, calls the "disease to please." I dare not ask the women in this room to raise their hand if they know what I'm talking about—the disease to please.

For all these girls, the demand to just say no is anathema. A pregnant teenager may have had to have sex to please a man upon whom she depends financially; she may fail to use contraception because the man either objects or makes it difficult by complaining that a condom reduces his pleasure, or he may threaten violence. She may have gotten pregnant in order to solidify a relationship, or to make a pledge of hope—the hope that there can be a better future, if not for herself, at least for her children. And society runs a moral risk by scapegoating teenage mothers. Even for middle-class girls who have not been abused, it's not so easy to look out for themselves. Our culture portrays sexually active girls as loose or cheap, thereby inhibiting girls from seeking information or services, such as contraception, for fear that this would be an acknowledgment that they want and plan on having sex.

Often girls are unable or unwilling to negotiate condom use or articulate their needs and desires because they've been taught by our culture to be docile and to please the man at all costs, or they fear accusations of unfaithfulness or intimidation, especially when partners are several years older.

Harvard professor Carol Gilligan, in her groundbreaking book *In a Different Voice,* wrote about the problems that ensue from rendering oneself selfless in order to have relationships. Professor Gilligan said, "Women's choices not to speak, or rather to disassociate themselves from what they themselves are saying, can be deliberate or unwitting, consciously chosen or enacted through the body by narrowing the passages that connect the voice with the breath and sound, by keeping the voice high in the head, so that it does not carry the depths of human feeling." Later she says, "The justification of these psychological processes in the name of love or relationships is equivalent to the justification of violence and violation in the name of morality."

Gilligan wrote that the problem of voicelessness becomes "central in women's development during the adolescent years when thought becomes reflective and the problem of interpretation thus enters the stream of development itself." And she adds that, "As girls become the carrier of unvoiced desires and unrealized possibilities, they are inevitably placed at considerable risk, even in danger."

When I first read *In a Different Voice,* the part about keeping the voice high in the head so that it doesn't carry the depth of human feelings, took my breath away. I've been there. I remembered my early years as a movie star and I looked at those early films. My voice was all high and thin, not expressing anything of what I was.

I have since gone back and tracked my growth as a woman by looking at my films chronologically and noting when my voice began to drop. It began with *Klute*—which was the first time I identified myself as a feminist. It was also when I won my first Oscar. My acting got better as I came to connect with myself, with my own *Klute.* I know what Professor Gilligan writes about, I know it in my skin, in my gut, as well as in my voice. But it has taken me into my sixties to own that voice and take what Gilligan calls "the road back from selflessness." And I went to the best schools—to Emma Willard School, the all-girl school where Gilligan did her research on the value of single-sex education for girls. God knows what would have happened if I had gone to a co-ed school. I would never have found my voice.

Anyway, in spite of that and my many advantages, I was conditioned to think that if I made my voice heard, I'd be selfish, no man would love me. That if I expressed desire or need, I would be a bad girl. So after a certain point, age eleven to be exact, I didn't know what I wanted anymore. I thought whatever the boy or man wanted was what I wanted. I remember when I auditioned in my early twenties for the movie *Splendor in the Grass,* the part that Natalie Wood eventually got, the renowned director Elia Kazan called me down to the footlights. He looked up at me and asked me, "Are you ambitious?" And I said, "No!" And in that half second, I saw the look of disappointment on his face and I knew I had lost the part. But good girls weren't ambitious. And I was still a good girl.

Women have made many strides in this country since Professor Gilligan wrote *In a Different Voice,* but we still have so far to go. I work with girls who have no advantages. I work with fourteen-year-olds who have already had their second child, girls who don't know their own bodies or what romance is. Or that they have a right to their own pleasure, a right to say no, or a right to have rights. And I see lives destroyed because of these things.

So many of the fine programs out there are less effective than they could be, or not effective at all because of gender issues and teachers' lack of knowledge and skills to address the problem. Many teachers and coaches, like most of us, suffer from unconscious, internalized gender prejudice that renders our work, if not our relationships, problematic.

We have the legal structures in place in this country that outlaw gender prejudice. We have, for example, Title IX, yet in violation of that, when a girl becomes pregnant, she is all too often forced to leave school or to go to an alternative school for troubled youth while the boy or man who impregnated her not only escapes censure but is almost never identified. We still have a culture of prejudice that allows girls to remain vulnerable and disadvantaged, and we still have a culture that teaches boys a distorted, often downright violent view of what it takes to be a man. This has to change, and we have to start young.

SPEAKING OUT FOR JUSTICE

The Legal Advocacy Fund of the American Association of University Women awarded Jane Fonda its 1999 Speaking Out for Justice Award, citing her work with the Georgia Campaign for Adolescent Pregnancy Prevention (G-CAPP) to reduce teen pregnancy.

If you study the animal world of which we are a part, the input for rearing children is not exclusively from parents. It's usually from parents, relatives, and community members who know the rules and feel a responsibility for the health and well being of the whole group. Just ask Jane Goodall. "It takes a village" is as true in the other part of the animal world as it is for *Homo sapiens.*

For human offspring, it used to be that kids lived in homes full of people of different generations. Parents, grandparents, boarders, nannies, and neighbors knew each other and looked out for each other. Kids were surrounded by adults whom they could observe, interact with, rebel against, and argue with. They were surrounded by adults of different generations in communities whose members felt a collective responsibility for the well being of all. What has happened is far deeper and more significant than "women in the

Speech prepared for the AAUW's Legal Advocacy Fund award ceremony, Washington, D.C., June 1999.

workplace." It's the whole fabric of family and community that has started to unravel.

The 1992 Carnegie Council on Adolescent Development Report called "A Matter of Time: Risk and Opportunity in the Non-School Hours" said that "many young people spend virtually all of their discretionary time without companionship or supervision by responsible adults."

In a *Los Angeles Times* article on June 12, a fifteen year-old freshman at Concord High School, Lindsay Spann, writes, "Shutup! Turn off the TV. Put down the newspaper. Stop drinking your scotch. Stop taking your Prozac. Put away your to-do list. Turn off your aromatherapy. Put away your cell phone. Turn off your pager, fax and computer. Stop your four-wheel-drive vehicle and refrain from looking in the mirror at your graying, balding hair and crow's-feet wrinkles. Look at us instead, your children." The article ends like this: "Take the time. We, your kids, shouldn't have to commit suicide or kill each other to get your attention."

Given their time alone, unsupervised, and too often uncared for, is it any wonder then that our kids are creating their own families, sometimes called gangs, their own rules and their own culture?

Loneliness, lack of structure, lack of consistent demonstrable love, lack of laps to sit on and arms to hold them is but one part of the story. It gets worse.

If you take a map of any state in this country that highlights the pockets of poverty in that state and then you overlay it with the areas where rates of adolescent pregnancy and births are high, you will find that generally they overlap. Eighty percent of young girls who have babies as adolescents were poor long before they became pregnant. Adolescent parenting is not the cause of poverty, it is a symptom of it.

Well, you might ask, isn't our economy booming? Isn't everyone doing better? You bet. By year 2000, the economic expansion will be the longest in this nation's history. There are more million-aires and billionaires than ever before, unemployment is at a twenty-nine-year low, the federal government has a record $64.7 billion budget surplus, Social Security has cut the poverty level for the elderly from over 20 percent in 1970 to the present 10 percent—and our kids are getting poorer.

In the United States, one in every four youth is impoverished; twice the rates of grown-ups. We spend fewer public resources on children than any other industrial nation in the world. In the last twenty years, child and youth poverty rose by 60 percent, whereas poverty among adults over the age of forty went down.

In 1995, a National Science Foundation–funded study by the Luxembourg Institute reported that of seventeen industrial nations the United States had the highest per capita and the highest child poverty rates.

Children living in poverty tend to be children who are discouraged, who see no future for themselves. Children with no future tend to do drugs, join gangs, drink, get pregnant, and sometimes act violently.

Not all poor children do, however. Some have a mother or father who stress the importance of education and make them know that they can do anything they set their minds to. These children, although poor, will be set out in life on an upward trajectory. They will be able to beat the odds, but the odds are against most poor kids.

Let's look at "my issue" of teen pregnancy. Girls are scolded for their promiscuous behavior, told to "just say no," blamed, thrown out of school, while the men who impregnated them usually remain anonymous and, certainly, blameless. Experts say, "What are we going to do with these girls?!"

What is rarely, if ever, mentioned in the same breath, even by people who devote their lives to the issue of preventing adolescent pregnancy, is who's getting them pregnant and how. Two-thirds of the pregnant and parenting teens in a mostly white Washington state sample had been sexually abused or raped. The victims averaged ten years old at the time of the abuse. Abusers averaged twenty-seven years old and most were adult male family members. These results were similar to those found in a 1989 study of mostly non-white Chicago teen mothers. Childhood sexual abuse was the single biggest predictor of teenage pregnancy over the past forty years, as a 1995 paper by the University of Chicago sociologists found.

Teen pregnancy shouldn't surprise us. One quarter of our American girls have been robbed of a sense of ownership of their own bodies, have never felt they had an option to say no, and the robbers were largely adult men.

And it's not over yet. A recent study reported in *Science* magazine found that 7 million children are victims of a severe violent act inflicted by parents. Parents! The adults they should be able to trust the most. These acts refer to more serious things than spanking or slapping, and include being kicked, bit, punched, beat up, burned or scalded, and threatened with a knife or gun, or actually having a knife or gun used on them. The United States leads the world in homicides of children. In 1995, the United States Advisory Board on Child Abuse and Neglect reported that "violence, mostly by adult parents and caretakers, kills 2,000 children and seriously injures 140,000 more per year." And the Child Welfare League of America reports that more children are murdered in the United States than in all of the world's twenty-six industrialized countries combined. Parents and caregivers do most of the murdering.

Ten years ago, the *American Journal of Psychiatry* published an investigation of fourteen juveniles on death row. Every one of them had suffered severe head trauma during childhood. All had deep psychiatric problems. Only two had managed to grow up without extreme physical or sexual abuse and five had undergone this at the hands of family members. Teen violence shouldn't surprise us. It's simply a reflection of the adult violence from which it stems.

Today, when Congress holds hearings on youth violence, where is the commensurate outcry about adult violence toward children? Our top officials, our media, even our experts aren't placing the problem of our adolescents within its true context: poverty, sexual abuse, violence at the hands of adults who they're supposed to trust, initiation to sex by rape, impregnation by older males, abandonment by adult fathers with little child support, and isolation from caring adults.

Yes, gun control is important and, yes, Hollywood should produce more responsible fare. But do we really believe that violence on the screen is more destructive to children than the blow of a fist or the lash of an extension cord?

I don't think America has an adolescent problem. We have an adult problem and we can't begin to solve it until we stop scapegoating the kids and face it square on.

SEX AND DESTINY

I wish my father could see me now. Lots of things about me caused him to scratch his head in bewilderment and this would have been one of them. How did his daughter end up speaking to an OB/GYN conference? But then his personal relationship to what goes on between a woman's legs probably didn't cause him to fret about the fact that so many women and girls don't understand their "down there" or how a woman's or girl's life is often determined by it—in bad ways as well as good, and that these issues start at puberty if not before.

Nor could he have suspected that his own daughter, whose puberty was particularly fraught, would, in her later years, find her calling in studying why this is so for so many girls and what can be done about it.

Most adolescent girls' puberty is fraught—fraught, because of sexual abuse, experienced by one out of four girls. Fraught, because of the cultural contradictions in this country which, on the one hand, tell girls that to be "good" they shouldn't have sex until they're married, that if they carry condoms they're asking for it. And, on the other hand, the media shows that to get a boyfriend they need to be sexy, to put out, to please. Fraught, because in the

Speech prepared for the Atlanta Obstetrical and Gynecological Society, Hotel Buckhead, Atlanta, Georgia, February 18, 2006.

midst of these contradictions, a teenager's burgeoning identity is so bound up with his or her sexuality.

All too often, girls have no one they can talk to except other fraught girls. It doesn't help that many of the adults who she's supposed to be able to turn to for answers and support don't really understand her.

It doesn't take long, when you're dealing with adolescents, to see that many adults who serve them don't like them very much. It's understandable. They're no longer the cuddly, sweet, needy children they once were. They're sullen, remote. They seem to think we're all intolerably dumb and don't want to listen to a thing we say. I saw a sign on a restaurant door once that said, "Quick, hire a teenager while they still know everything."

Many of us, including the professionals who serve them, aren't trained to understand the very specific ways adolescents are different developmentally, cognitively, from children and adults; how gender stereotypes and abuse and poverty or racism affects them and the way they handle their emerging sexuality.

I lost my mother when I was twelve. Like many teens, I had so many issues about sex and my "down there." I was convinced that, when God was handing out vaginas, I'd gotten a faulty one. When I was fourteen—in the 1950s—Christine Jorgensen underwent the first highly publicized man-to-woman transgendering and I was convinced that, like her, I'd been born the wrong sex . . . pretty heavy stuff.

Of course, even if my mother had been alive, I wouldn't have been able to talk to her about such things. I'd tried that once with sorry results. But I had a very smart stepmother who sent me to an OB/GYN as soon as I got my period.

His name was Dr. Lazar Margulies and he happened to be the pioneer of the now famous spiral-shaped, plastic IUD. I was one of the first to use one and it served me well for many years. But it wasn't so much the IUD that had such an effect on me. It was Dr.

Margulies himself. He took his time with me. I was able to confess my fears and shame and he really listened without judging or laughing, as if it was the most natural thing in the world.

I have often wondered what would have become of me had I not been fortunate enough to find a doctor like that. I sometimes imagine that I'm a poor girl of color with all the same fears and issues but no health care and no access to such a physician—how dangerously I might have acted out in an attempt to prove I was just like everyone else.

Then there was the issue of gender and self-esteem. Like a lot of girls, I learned early on that to be validated, I had to have a boyfriend or later, be with a man—preferably an alpha male—and to ensure he loved me I had to please him, be what he wanted. I want to say this because you might think that girls and women like me who are capable and successful in other aspects of their lives— socially, professionally—aren't likely to give up their voices when it comes to sex. Not true. Our culture teaches girls to try to be popular by having boyfriends and to be malleable, to please. And unfortunately, girls' standing among their peers equates with where their boyfriends are on the hierarchy of testosterone.

Girls who acknowledge their own physical desires are considered bad girls in our culture and this puts them at real risk. Sex becomes something they do to please someone else, without any embodiment of their own passions. There is little consequence in giving away what you don't value or acknowledge. They betray their hearts and bodies so as to be popular, to fit in, to get asked out on that second date. They are made to feel that being in relationship with a boy is more important than being in relationship with themselves. This inevitably causes psychic pain and to mask the pain of performing sexual acts that deep down they don't want to do, they will often get drunk or stoned or pop pills. They go through their adolescence alienated from their own desires, never learning to really listen to their bodies, never paying attention to their breathing and what it is telling them about the presence or absence of desire and fear. Research has shown that girls who have agency over their bodies and own their voice of desire are far less likely to act out sexually or engage in risky behavior.

It's almost impossible to have agency over your body if you've been sexually abused as a young girl, which, as I said, is the case for one out of four girls. In other words, it's an epidemic! Childhood sexual abuse has been the biggest predictor of teenage pregnancy over the past forty years. This is because abuse isn't just a physical trauma, it's a form of brainwashing. The girl feels guilt, often for the rest of her life, unless she receives proper therapy. By the way, this is greatly minimized if someone believes her. She learns that the only thing about her of value is her sexuality and that becomes the way she acts out to validate herself.

Often, it's the most extreme cases that teach us the lessons we're supposed to learn. One day, more than ten years ago, when I was just beginning to think about starting the Georgia Campaign for Adolescent Pregnancy Prevention, I was touring the maternity ward of a county hospital near Albany, Georgia, and was taken to a cubicle where a fourteen-year-old girl was in labor with her second child. Before I went in, the nurse told me that the girl lived in a tar-paper shack with no indoor plumbing. I looked down into her dark, expressionless eyes that stared right up at me, as though challenging me to judge her. I wish I had kissed her. She needed someone to take her in their arms and not let go for about twenty years. I wondered if anyone ever had—except for during sex.

I have subsequently learned that 60 percent of teen moms her age have been victims of early sexual abuse. I'm certain that fourteen-year-old was one of them. I knew that no one should judge such a girl. I also realized that giving her condoms wouldn't be enough. What if I had supplied her with six years' worth of contraception, enough to bring her to twenty years of age? What else did she have in her life besides the child? How could I tell her not to have any more unless I could promise her a future that would motivate her to use contraceptives?

In Georgia, every year, there are 800 pregnancies to girls ages ten to thirteen. *Children!* What could "just say no" mean to girls like these? What could "abstinence till marriage" mean? What does it mean that there are OB/GYNs in this state who believe that a girl can't get pregnant from a rape?

That fourteen-year-old girl in Albany having her second child? I will bet that if she *was* examined by an OB/GYN prior to her first pregnancy, the doctor would not have known how to identify sexual abuse, and on the outside chance they picked up on it, they wouldn't have known what to do with the information or how to help the girl and get the perpetrator behind bars.

That is why, almost five years ago, we opened the Jane Fonda Center at Emory School of Medicine to address a myriad of training needs around adolescent reproductive health and sexuality. Physicians, social workers and nurses expressed the need for more training in identifying and treating physical and sexual abuse and donated their time to help us develop an annual conference with nationally recognized faculty. A committee of OB/GYN and pediatric faculty from Emory and Morehouse also helped us develop a curriculum that addresses sexually transmitted disease prevention and treatment, family planning, adolescent-friendly services, cultural competency and adolescents' legal rights to access reproductive health services. Since the inception of the project, over 600 physicians and 500 mid-level providers in Georgia have received at least one educational component.

I often think about that fourteen-year-old girl in Albany. I imagine her coming into a clinic, being hurried into an examining room and asked to spread her legs for a pelvic exam. I would expect she'd run away like a scared rabbit and never come back. Or she'd experience what many girls her age have described to me, being judged by the staff of the health clinic. That's another thing that can cause these girls, already victims, to stop seeking medical care.

What I have learned is that clinical services for adolescents must be designed for adolescents. Their needs are different from grown-ups. They need time to build a trusting relationship with the service provider; they need time to get their myriad questions answered. They need to talk about feelings, not just the plumbing, but feelings. What does intimacy mean? What should a real relationship feel like? They need doctors and nurses who can identify sexual abuse and do a one-time interview that can hold up in court. They need to be seen as whole people, not just as problems that exist from the waist to the knees.

Some might think that providing these services to adolescents is usurping the role of parents, but research shows that most parents *want* help with their kids in these areas. These are not easy things to be articulate about in ways that kids can really hear and internalize, and if they sense even the slightest wisp of judgment, they're history.

One place where state-of-the-art teen services are all found is the Adolescent Reproductive Health Clinic at Grady Hospital. In 2005, the clinic served over 2,800 adolescents, boys as well as girls. It's hard to get young men to come to a clinic and then to come back. At the Grady Clinic last year, some 350 adolescent males made over 500 visits to the weekly clinic held for males only. They usually get brought in the first time by their girlfriends, but the clinic offers free sports physicals and that encourages boys to come back and then they develop that indispensable relationship with the doctor or nurse or the male counselor.

The clinic sees girls as young as twelfth and thirteen with sexually transmitted infections such as genital herpes or chlamydia. Some young ones are actually needing hysterectomies. When very young teens that are sexually active come into the clinic, it raises a red flag for staff to screen very carefully for any history of sexual abuse.

What is unique about this clinic, and what teens say they like most about coming there, is having their own counselors. Unlike health care in the private sector where you have your own doctor that sees you consistently, in the public sector you see whatever doctor is available. Having a caring adult who understands adolescents and having that person be available to them at clinic visits or by telephone makes the teens feel special. Most importantly, they don't have to tell their life story to someone different every time they need service.

I talked earlier about the gender stereotypes that endanger adolescent girls. But what about the boys? Many, if not most, young men grow up believing that to be a man they have to dominate somebody or get a girl pregnant. This takes on real poignancy in the case of poor young men.

Along with the clinical care that you provide young people, hope and healthy self-esteem are the best contraceptives, believing that their future would be compromised by early parenthood and other risky behaviors. This is above-the-waist work. This means being in it for the long haul. There is no quick fix. This is what informs the work that the Georgia Campaign for Adolescent Pregnancy Prevention does.

In closing, let me say why this issue of teen pregnancy and parenting should matter to all of us. Remember these statistics when you want to make the case to some doubting Thomas: had teen pregnancy rates in Georgia not gone down 27 percent between 1991 and 2002, 35,000 additional children would have been born to teen mothers and nearly 10,000 more children under the age of six would have been living in poverty in 2002.

As a result of Georgia's decline in teen births during these years, we've seen 3 percent improvement in the state's poverty rate for children under age six and an 8 percent improvement in the proportion of children under age six living in a single-mother household. Teen pregnancy is the cause of intergenerational transfer of poverty. Preventing teen pregnancy is one of the most direct and effective ways states can reduce poverty and improve overall child well-being.

Then there's the fact that it costs Georgia's taxpayers $1.2 billion in state and federal funds each year to support families begun by teen mothers. It costs far, far less to prevent the pregnancy in the first place. Yet funding to do just that—after-school programs, teen clinics, school counselors, proper training, Medicaid—is being cut back because so much money is going to the military. Children and family services have to fight tooth and nail for every penny. This is the height of shortsightedness. Help us advocate for funding for these services.

Finally, I pray that you, who have the chance to intersect with adolescents on the most intimate level, will not just provide them with contraception and information. I hope that you will connect with them in love, compassion and full understanding of the reality of their lives. You may be the only one who does and that can be transformational. It was for me.

REAL BOYS AND GOOD GIRLS

I have been working with young people here for six years and previously ran a children's camp in California for fifteen years. When I began this work, I thought that the solution to adolescent pregnancy was more contraception and sexuality education. Yes, these things are critical, but the youth my organization works with often *want* to get pregnant or they lack the motivation to avoid getting pregnant. It does take motivation. You have to be very real clear about what you want, to use contraception effectively. And you have to see a future for yourself that you know would be compromised if you had a baby. If you don't see a future for yourself, or if you have no self-concept beyond being someone's girlfriend, then all you'll care about is pleasing and you'll lack the motivation to stick to your guns.

Middle-class girls get abortions. Poor girls have their babies because they see no other alternative. So in our work we have to help young girls see a future.

Another important thing is helping parents feel okay about themselves. Most adolescent parents were children of adolescent parents—it's cyclical. Some young people are ready to be good

Speech prepared for the Minnesota Organization on Adolescent Pregnancy, Prevention and Parenting, May 2001.

parents but most are not, and it's hard to be a good parent if you haven't had good parenting. So, how to break the cycle?

I discovered an answer in Chicago. It's called the Doula Project and is the creation of an organization called Ounce of Prevention. Evaluations of the doula program shows a significant reduction in child abuse, maternal substance abuse and second pregnancies. But we at G-CAPP believe this program will prove itself as a long-term strategy for *primary* pregnancy prevention as well. We believe that, due to the more profound and nurturing parenting they receive as babies, the children, when they grow up, will not repeat the cycle and become adolescent parents themselves.

Another thing I've learned through my work in Georgia is the relationship between dropping out of school and adolescent pregnancy. School failure is an indicator that a young person has given up. Rather than being the cause of school drop out, pregnancy usually follows it. Dr. Michael Carrera, founder and director of the Children's Aid Society's Adolescent Pregnancy Prevention program, says that the best thing a parent can do to prevent a child from becoming a parent too soon is to keep her in school and doing well.

School failure can often be predicted very early on in a child's school life. Many cities are concerned about the increasing number of children starting school unprepared and unable to hold a pencil or listen. These are the children who are almost guaranteed to become tomorrow's dropouts.

I discovered Educare, also in Chicago, also run by Ounce of Prevention. It represents a coming together of social work and early child development and takes a holistic approach to family service by offering individual and group therapy, counseling, health care, with staff who are highly trained. Two of these centers are being brought to Atlanta. What I've been seeing in my work in Georgia is that we have to create a continuum from birth through adolescence that will help kids grow up resilient.

Recently, when hearing about these programs, one of G-CAPP's board members who is a nationally recognized expert in the field of adolescent pregnancy prevention asked, "Why would you want to offer these things to the young mothers? That's rewarding them for their mistakes."

I was stunned! If this person could ask this, he who should know better, what do others think! And I realized that an important task lies ahead of us: to educate the public about the reality of girls' lives.

Too many people assume that girls have considerable autonomy over their lives in general and their sex lives in particular. But, instead of demonizing young mothers, we need to recognize that their behavior is not always an expression of their free will. A pregnant teenager may have had to have sex to please a man she depends on financially. She may fail to use contraception because the man either objects or makes it difficult by complaining that a condom reduces his pleasure or he may threaten violence.

Even for middle-class girls who have not been abused, it is not so easy to look out for themselves. Our culture portrays sexually active girls as "loose" or "cheap," thereby inhibiting girls from seeking information or services such as contraception for fear that this would be an acknowledgment that they want and plan on having sex. Often girls are unable or unwilling to negotiate condom use because they have been taught by our culture to be docile and to please the man at all costs or they fear accusations of unfaithfulness or intimidation, especially when partners are several years older.

When our culture forbids girls to own their voice of desire they are put at great risk. Sex becomes something they do to please someone else, without any embodiment of their own passions. There is little consequence in giving away what you do not value or acknowledge.

Society runs a moral risk by scapegoating teenage mothers. Instead we need to approach the problem with understanding and compassion, seeking ways to break the cycle. This means making it easier for young mothers to stay in school, helping them develop tools for good parenting and providing their children with therapeutic child care. Most mothers want to do right by their children and are personally empowered when they learn how. To improve the lives of the girls and their children is to reduce the likelihood of repeat pregnancies and, in the long run, as I have said, to improve the chances that the children of these girls will not become adolescent parents themselves.

I've discovered there is another misconception that puts girls at risk and that is the idea that male and female adolescents form a homogenous group with common needs and interests. We fail to recognize how gender makes the experience of adolescence different for girls than for boys. Adolescence is a time of heightened vulnerability for girls, a time of silence, passivity and devaluation, while for boys it is a time of increased power and social validity.

In an effort to address this profound issue, I am working with Professor Carol Gilligan and her colleagues at the Harvard Graduate School of Education as well as other researchers from Wellesley, NYU, and elsewhere to develop curricula for middle-school-aged girls and, beginning after the first of the year, with their male counterparts, to address curricula appropriate for elementary-school-aged boys. These curricula will address the cultural conventions of manhood and womanhood, the meanings of being a "real boy" and "good girl," which are so detrimental to human development.

Work done by Gilligan at Harvard over the last three decades has confirmed and expanded previous research that showed that girls in early adolescence, roughly between the ages of eleven and fifteen, appear to show signs of emotional distress: depression, eating disorders, loss of vitality. Analysis of the research shows that at this developmental stage, when pressures around establishing femininity are heightened, girls shut down their voice, hide what they know and feel, in order to be in relationships as defined by our culture: "don't be too strong, too outspoken, too sexual, too aggressive." In other words, they lose relationship with themselves in order to be in relationship with boys. This, as I know only too well within my own life, doesn't end with adolescence but is a pattern that, unless consciously broken, can continue throughout our lives. We can be strong women professionally, politically, but our most intimate relationship is where loss of voice shows up.

For boys, this loss of relationship happens roughly between the ages of five and seven, a time which coincides with the start of formal schooling. At this age boys are seen as experiencing signs of emotional stress, especially depression, learning disorders, speech impediments, and are more likely to manifest signs of out-of-control behavior. Currently in the United States, one in ten boys this age are on Ritalin.

For many years these behaviors were attributed to biology—"boys will be boys" and "girls are just experiencing hormonal surges." But recently we have learned that psychological and cultural factors play a more significant role. In addition, the success of programs that encourage girls' interest and performance in math, science and sports and interventions which help young men get in touch with their emotional lives argue against a simple biological determinism.

Research draws attention to a gendered pattern in these crises: whereas girls, when pressed to choose between maintaining their integrity, their voice, and having relationships, will choose having relationships, boys are likely to stand with their independence, their voices, and turn their backs on relationships. Both choices are detrimental to human development, to creativity, resiliency and human vitality. One represents sacrificing integrity, or self, for the sake of relationships, the other represents loss of relationships for the sake of integrity. Neither represents relationships in any meaningful sense. And relationships are at the core of human development. Relationships are the oxygen of the psyche.

It is difficult for us adults to effectively help young girls and boys regain their full human capacity to be relational unless we ourselves have addressed our own deeply ingrained gender issues, the ways in which gender norms have woven themselves into our very DNA. I am here to tell you that it is an essential ingredient to the work we do and that it is never too late. The Harvard project is also working to develop processes that can help adults with this transformation.

To fully address these issues that impact youth, and to do it sustainably, we need statewide policies and we need national policies. This isn't easy, especially now. The mentality that seems to be prevailing in Washington, D.C., is the belief that women shouldn't work, that people are poor because they are lazy, that girls who get pregnant are bad girls who should be punished.

I know you agree with me that most youth are responsible, capable and deserving of societal supports and protection. But convincing decision makers of this is difficult in the absence of a natural sympathy for adolescents and a clearer picture of their experience. And because young people do not constitute an organized and vocal constituency with the social and economic power to lobby on their own behalf, the lack of governmental commitments to adolescents goes largely unchallenged.

If we can do right by our children during all their formative stages, we will have gone far to reduce adolescent pregnancy and we will have a very different nation.

I hope I have given you some food for thought and that, as a consequence, you will think of ways that your institution can partner with your community to address these issues.

PREVENTING TEEN
PREGNANCY

All my adult life I've been fascinated by our ability to experience transformation. No other animal, at least that we know
of, can evolve upward, spiritually, psychologically, emotionally the
way we can. Perhaps my fascination with this comes from my having been an actress for so long. All the best roles are characters that
experience change and so we actors pay a lot of attention to what
triggers human change, what that looks like and feels like. It isn't
statistics and facts or words coming at us, like "You better not
do that anymore!" that trigger transformation. Transformation is
about feelings. It comes when your heart is touched. The feeling of
doing something good and being respected for it; of discovering a
valuable talent you didn't know you had; of being seen and heard
when you're not used to it. The feeling of being held and discovering that you're loveable. These are examples of catalysts for positive
human transformation.

For fifteen years, together with my former husband, Tom Hayden, I had a summer camp for children in California. The campers
were from all economic backgrounds and races, and during that
time I learned a lot about transformation, like when children
who've lacked contact are held and feel a warm, loving, human

Speech prepared for the National Press Club, Washington, D.C., June 24, 1998.

touch without sexual overtones. I learned how transformative it is for children to set goals and achieve them and be acknowledged for it, for children to have an adult to talk to who cared for them and knew how to listen and told them the truth in an age-appropriate way. I was surprised at how many of the hundreds who came through the camp seemed to have lacked that. I learned the extent that deprivation can exist among children of the rich and the emotional richness that can exist among the very poor. I learned the importance of children who had everything being exposed to children who had very little and vice versa. I asked one child from a particularly deprived background why the camp had affected her so much. She thought for a minute and then said, "I'd never met anyone before who thought about the future."

We adults have to think about what the future will be like if we don't address the problems that cause young people to have babies and if we fail to understand why so many of our youth don't see a future for themselves.

For a long time, several decades perhaps, adolescent parenthood has provided conservatives and liberals alike with a convenient scapegoat. Age is easier to talk about than race, gender and class. We've blamed poverty and welfare on what we've called an "epidemic" of kids having babies and having them when they aren't married. We've blamed unplanned pregnancies on the young people's apparent lack of responsible decision making: "If teenagers could just discipline themselves more, all would be well." In doing this, we've conveniently overlooked the fact that 60 percent of *adult* pregnancies in the U.S. aren't planned. It's not an epidemic of teenagers having out-of-wedlock babies. It's *adult* women having out-of-wedlock babies that's epidemic. Two-thirds of unwed mothers in America are not teens, and two-thirds of the fathers of the babies born to teen mothers are adult men.

When it comes to out-of-wedlock, unplanned babies, adults provide poor role models. Instead of asking ourselves why adolescents who have unplanned babies out of wedlock are so different, we should be asking why they are behaving so similarly to everyone else.

And, just as an aside, the national teen birthrate was at its highest back in 1957, those puritanical good old days that never really were. Girls under fifteen years have been having children at about the same rate for most of the past seventy years. What was different back then was a higher likelihood that the youngsters would end up marrying and the fact that children weren't as poor then as they are today. More about that in a minute.

Recently, we've learned that since 1991 there has been a 12 percent reduction nationally in the rate of adolescent pregnancy. Among African American girls, it's 21 percent. So, you may ask, "If adults are doing it too and there's no epidemic and the rates are going down, why should we still be concerned?" Here are some reasons: because the number is still way too high; close to half a million girls give birth each year in this country and we have the highest rates of any industrialized nation. We should be concerned because far too many children begin life at a disadvantage and if they have a child it becomes harder to take advantage of whatever opportunities and lucky breaks come along.

A youngster's earnings tend to go up if there is no child. Children of teen moms are at greater risk for abuse and neglect. Boys born to teens are 13 percent more likely to be incarcerated. High school completion is lower if the student has a child. Even poor girls can leave public housing sooner if they have no children. Fathers tend to stay in school longer if they have no child. Children of adolescent parents are more impaired in cognitive development and have more behavioral problems.

This nation cannot afford to have a growing underclass of antisocial, psychologically and developmentally impaired, unskilled, angry young people born to discouraged, ill-prepared, unskilled and angry teenage parents. And we cannot afford to ignore them with the old it's-not-happening-in-my-community mentality. For these children will become part of the future that will be shared by all our children. Whether another child grows up to be a doctor or a drug peddler may have great bearing on your child. If another child becomes a social worker instead of a gangbanger, the world will be a little safer for your child. We are all interconnected in this. We can't write any children off.

If we are to succeed at reducing adolescent pregnancy, we need to start by defining it and understanding it more accurately. We can begin by acknowledging that adolescent pregnancy is an *adult* problem. Its causes are adult-driven and the transformations that must occur if it is to be solved must be brought about by adults.

What are these adult-driven causes?

First, there's poverty. Rather than being the *cause* of social and economic ills, adolescent pregnancy is a *symptom* of those ills. For example, it's very rare that adolescent moms are well-to-do youngsters who had babies and then went on the dole. When affluent girls get pregnant, they more often will have an abortion. The ones that have their babies make up fewer than one-fifth of adolescent births. On the other hand, nearly 80 percent of adolescent mothers lived in poverty or near poverty long before they became pregnant. Whereas it used to be America's elderly who were the poor, now it's our children. Twenty percent of America's children live in poverty. Poverty, and the discouragement that often accompanies it, is a precursor to adolescent parenthood. For poor girls and boys who see no future for themselves, having a child can seem like an option, a way to attain adult status, to win love, gain a second chance, to have someone that belongs to them and depends on them.

The United States has the highest rate of child poverty of any industrialized country. Overall, 40 percent of America's poor are children. Overall, 48 percent of American children make up the chronically poor. The public pays for poverty one way or another and it is expensive, financially, socially, morally and spiritually. Larger sums are spent on corporate welfare in America, on corporate tax breaks and subsidies, than on welfare for the poor.

Not all kids who are poor get pregnant. If there is a parent or surrogate parent in the home who is close to the child and lets them know the importance of a good education and that they can be somebody, that young person, though poor, is going to be less discouraged, more motivated, less likely to get pregnant and be more able to seek and seize opportunities when they come along. Those parents deserve all the credit we can give them because poverty brings with it so many interrelated problems including food insecurity, lack of proper nutrition and health care, tension, alcohol or drug abuse, physical abuse—things that make it extremely difficult to be a good parent.

The second cause of adolescent pregnancy is lack of parental involvement in, and supervision of, a child's life. Many studies have shown that when children feel a strong emotional connection to their parents from early on, when the parent or parents communicate clear values and give the child clear parameters, risk behaviors of all kinds including early pregnancy go way down. Adolescent mothers tend to be daughters of adolescent mothers who, all too often, have not learned how to be appropriate parents. Thus the problem becomes generational. I have to say here that I know that many teens have made very good mothers and that the experience of motherhood gave them the wherewithal to turn their lives around. But they are the exception and the odds are against them.

A survey by the National Campaign to Prevent Teen Pregnancy showed that teens *want* their parents to talk more with them about a lot of issues such as contraception, dating, sexually transmitted diseases and when to say no to sex. Seven out of ten teens said they were ready to listen but their parents thought they were not ready to hear. Parents, it appears, don't believe their kids will pay any attention to what they say on these matters. Kids say they would.

We're suffering from sexual schizophrenia here and all of us, including our children, are the losers. Talking about sex, it seems, requires more intimacy than actually doing it since a majority of adults are uncomfortable talking with their children about relationships, intimacy, sex and how to avoid pregnancy, AIDS and the other illnesses associated with unsafe sex. Nationally, 84 percent of mothers across social and economic lines say they need and want help communicating with their children about these issues.

Into this parental vacuum pour powerful messages from the media and from peers, leaving children without the skills and information to combat them. They are bombarded daily with provocative sexual stimuli where sex is expressed through commercialism, politics and pathology rather than as healthy, beautiful and responsible human development. A Harris poll says that the average number of incidents of sexual behavior seen by teens on afternoon television is 57 per week or 2,969 per year. For prime-time television it came to 7,438 per year, with no references made to sexually transmitted diseases or safe sex. The "Leave It to Beaver" generation has given birth to the *Beavis and Butt-head* generation and can't seem to come to grips with the realities of this new world.

Parents say they need help talking about sex with their children. Youth organizations have to pay more attention to this. Advocates for Youth has booklets on programs and videos that can help parents. I wish that I had had those tools when my children were at the asking age. The National Campaign to Prevent Teen Pregnancy has prepared a pamphlet called "Ten Tips for Parents to Help Their Children Avoid Teen Pregnancy."

A third antecedent to adolescent pregnancy and parenthood are dysfunctional communities where there are unstable populations, where people don't know their neighbors, don't help each other out and where there are a lot of drugs and violence. Try telling a boy in a community like that not to get girls pregnant. Most of them don't think they'll live much past twenty. What other legacy have they to leave besides a child or, better yet from their point of view, many children?

Claire Brindis, a researcher from the University of California, San Francisco, told of a young girl who cried when learning that she wasn't pregnant. When asked why she was upset she replied, "My boyfriend will be mad. He doesn't think he'll live long and he wants a baby who can grow up and take care of his mom." Community violence is exacerbated by media violence. We've heard it before but it bears repeating: teens watch television an average of twenty-one hours a week. By age eighteen, teens will have seen as many as 18,000 televised murders and 800 suicides. Three major studies concluded that higher levels of viewing violence on TV are correlated with increased acceptance of aggressive attitudes and increased aggressive behavior.

A fourth cause of teen pregnancy is school failure. School failure and dropout are signs that a youngster has become discouraged and is giving up on him/herself. These youngsters will often turn to parenthood as a second chance, a way to succeed at something.

A fifth cause is gender bias that values girls and women in terms of their sexuality and fertility rather than as whole human beings. After all these years, too much in our culture makes girls feel they should be subservient to the male, which can lead to girls and women who are victims of brutalization feeling that it is what they deserve. Gender bias is one reason why pregnancy has been viewed as the girl's problem, leaving out the role of the sperm. It's her fault if she gets pregnant, yet if a girl carries condoms, society views her as a predatory "bad girl" who was planning to have sex. Being carried away in a moment of passion is more acceptable. On the other hand, if a boy carries condoms he's viewed as a "good boy" who is prepared.

Recently I've learned about "side girls." A boy will have his main squeeze and then several girls on the side. These side girls, as they are called, seem to accept their position as though it's normal and wait in the hope that in time they'll be moved up the ladder. Too often, boys define their masculinity in terms of having a lot of women, sowing a lot of seeds and even roughing up the women. These values are passed down through the generations and are internalized by men and women alike.

Another factor that has a significant relationship to early pregnancy and parenthood is sexual abuse and it is far more prevalent than most of us realize. Studies have estimated one out of four American females have been sexually abused and estimates are that less than 10 percent of sexual abuse is reported to the police. Four in ten women who have sex before the age of fifteen report their first sexual experience as coerced. Sexual abuse has long-term psychological effects that are difficult to heal. The message that is emblazoned into the heart of an abuse victim is that her only worth is her sex, that her body doesn't belong to her, that she has no control over herself. The "just say no" message to abuse victims is incomprehensible. When has saying no ever been an option for them? Sexual abuse survivors often begin voluntary sexual relationships earlier and are more likely to become pregnant before the age of eighteen. One study found one-half to two-thirds of pregnant teens reported sexual abuse histories. Sexual abuse eradicates the very skills that are needed for girls to protect themselves from pregnancy, sexually transmitted diseases and AIDS.

Finally, I come to two factors related to adolescent pregnancy prevention that cause the most controversy: Sexuality education and reproductive health services.

Far too many young people today don't understand that the new feelings they experience during puberty are normal. They don't know enough about how their bodies work, how babies are made and how to protect themselves. For these reasons a solid majority of every regional and demographic group in the country supports requiring schools to teach sex education, yet only twenty-two states plus Washington, D.C., and Puerto Rico, require sexuality education, only fifteen states and Washington, D.C., and Puerto Rico monitor its implementation and only twelve states, Washington, D.C., and Puerto Rico require teachers of sex education to be certified.

On top of the less than optimal manner in which states are choosing to implement, or not implement, sex education, there is a debate raging over two different versions of what sex education should entail. One version is the abstinence-only or chastity approach, which holds that the only acceptable message is for youth to remain abstinent until they are married. They permit no information about contraception. In fact, contraception is only discussed in terms of its failure rate, which, by the way, is 2 percent if properly used and over 9 percent if not properly used. Some of the curricula perpetuate medical inaccuracies and are fear-based, focusing on the negative consequences of premarital sex. It would be interesting to know what percent of children who are being steeped in these scarey messages grow up with dysfunctional sex lives.

The other version of sex education is called abstinence-plus, and the curricula are more comprehensive. Proponents of this approach believe it's not the "no" part of the "just say no" message that's wrong, it's the "just." Abstinence-plus curricula begin by encouraging abstinence and stressing why it is the surest way to avoid pregnancy and AIDS, etc., but since two-thirds of high school students have sex before graduating, and given the high rates of sexual abuse, they also provide medically accurate information about sex that includes information on contraception as well as refusal skills.

No rigorous scientific evaluation has yet found evidence that the abstinence-plus message and availability of contraception hastens the onset of sexual activity, the frequency of sex or the numbers of partners. In fact, two recent studies out of Washington and New York show just the opposite. There is evidence that abstinence-plus programs, if properly taught by trained teachers, can be effective at delaying first intercourse and promoting the safer sex practices needed to avoid pregnancy and AIDS. No such evidence exists for the abstinence-only approach.

I do not mean to imply here that stressing abstinence isn't a good thing. This message may very well be persuasive for younger youth who are not already sexually active. One recent study showed that the abstinence-only approach, when it provides accurate information, does not portray sex in a negative light and was not moralistic, had a short-term impact on younger teens. The effectiveness diminished with longer-term follow-up. In spite of the recent Kaiser Family Foundation study which found that 74 percent of teens say it is considered a "good thing to make a conscious decision not to have sex until some later time" and the term "secondary virginity" notwithstanding, it's been proven very difficult to get already sexually active youth, especially boys, to become abstinent.

The majority of Americans support the abstinence-plus approach. When asked, "Do you think that sex ed programs in public schools should provide children with age appropriate information about how pregnancy occurs, how to prevent pregnancy, and how to prevent sexually transmitted diseases?" 87 percent respond yes, while only 24 percent of Americans support the abstinence-only approach.

We can learn from other countries. Our pregnancy rate is twice that of the United Kingdom, where age-appropriate sexuality education begins in kindergarten and continues through twelfth grade.

The other controversial issue concerning pregnancy prevention has to do with adolescents' access to family planning clinics. The number of sexually active adolescents had doubled between 1970 and 1990. To date, 12 million teens are sexually active. Opponents of publicly funded contraception appear to justify their opposition by pointing out that federal programs, until recently, have slowed but not reversed the rising rates of adolescent pregnancy. They use this to label these programs as failures. They ignore the fact that, while there has been a doubling of the population of sexually active adolescents, there has been no doubling of the pregnancy rate, and publicly funded family planning services was the main reason why. These programs are an immense success story. Yet, in spite of this, federal funding of family planning services dropped sharply from 400 million in 1980 to 250 million in 1990.

The Census Bureau estimates that by the year 2005 the percentage of youth in the United States ages ten to nineteen will increase by 13 percent. If federal funding for effective adolescent pregnancy prevention programs and services doesn't increase proportionately, we are going to be facing even bigger problems.

Most Americans, 72 percent of them, support government provision of family planning services to anyone who needs them. In one year alone, according to the Alan Guttmacher Institute, publicly subsidized contraceptive services averted 285,800 adolescent pregnancies. For every dollar invested in publicly subsidized family planning services, the taxpayers saved three dollars in Medicaid-related costs. To put it another way, and using the Guttmacher formula, if the money allocated in 1996 to the abstinence-only curricula had been invested instead in publicly funded family planning services for adolescents, the savings in Medicaid costs for pregnancy-related health care and medical care for newborns would have been $177 million. Most Americans would agree with columnist E. J. Dionne Jr., who said in a recent *Washington Post* article, "Teaching clear values is essential to helping teens avoid early sexual activity and pregnancy, but birth control is needed as a backup."

It's not that contraception and family planning clinics alone will solve the adolescent pregnancy problem. Too often, the clinics are not open during hours, and on days, when youth can get to them.

Their waiting lists can be months long, and too often they aren't kid-friendly; staff are overworked and sometimes judgmental. To optimally serve adolescents, clinics need to do active youth outreach and have specially trained staff to counsel youth and do consistent follow-up. The most successful clinics are ones where youth develop a consistent and trusting relationship with a staff member.

G-CAPP, the campaign I chair, advocates mandatory counseling that starts by discussing abstinence, why it's cool and why it's the safest alternative, that encourages and when needed facilitates parental involvement instead of the traditional approach, which helps the youth choose a contraceptive and shows them how to use it. The youth-appropriate approach would ask about the relationship: "Is it a trusting one? How does he or she treat you? Are there other partners? How do you feel about the relationship?" Clinics should be encouraged and funding should be provided to have males on staff, thereby encouraging boys and men to come in. When fathers are involved with their children, whether or not they live with the mother and whether or not they are able to provide child support, the children fare better and risk behaviors like premature pregnancy and parenting are reduced.

We should love our children more and make sure that our state and national policies reflect that love. Young people in America today face new and immense social and economic challenges: they face a shrinking job market, live in communities that are hostile for growing children and there is lack of true concern for the well-being of minorities. It's amazing that they are doing as well as they are with so little help. In our work we should build on the considerable strengths and assets of our youth.

Statewide efforts should not ignore the critical role of advocacy. Opponents of the comprehensive approaches are in the minority but they are heavily organized, are attempting to take over school boards, county health departments, state legislatures, and Congress. They are the voices that are being heard. On behalf of America's children; every state, every community, every parent and every young person and organization has to think about how you can help mobilize the energies and support of the silent majority in your area who agree with the comprehensive approaches and help reach out to and educate the ones who are unsure. Remember, an 80 percent friend isn't a 20 percent enemy.

Part IV

For Women (and Men)

ALL THE JOYS
OF A WOMAN IN CHILDBIRTH

I was there at the time of the heaviest bombing, ten to fifteen air raids a day in and outside Hanoi. I saw women and children in the hospitals with their bodies mutilated by these weapons. The thing that made such an impression—and it's hard for me to say it without sounding like I'm romanticizing—I expected to find haggard, frightened, downtrodden people, and I found radiant, brave, totally optimistic people. They sang a lot, touched each other a lot, had lots of babies and wrote poetry. The last phrase of a poem to Nixon written by their national poet says, "We will fight you with all the joys of a woman in childbirth." This captures for me what I sensed there. The people were prepared to undergo all kinds of hardships, but they had what seemed a powerful certainty about their future and were not afraid to bring children into it. . . .

If you're fortunate enough to be in this country, it's an unbearable pain to know so many people are suffering because of the United States. Over half the political prisoners in South Vietnam are women. A lot have given birth in prison to babies who are dying, starving. We have poems by women in prison about hearing the cries of babies after their mothers have been beaten and can't

"Vietnamese Women's Example Overcame Jane Fonda's Cynicism," *Detroit Free Press,* September 13, 1972.

nurse them. People ask why we have so much energy. I just keep thinking of these women in South Vietnam, reading their poems that have so much courage. Their assumption is that if American women knew what's really happening in Vietnam, we would act. . . .

PUTTING WOMEN
AT THE CENTER

When a woman is educated, when she is able to earn some money outside her home, money over which she has control, when she has access to credit and training, she gains status, she wants and needs fewer children, and she can negotiate family planning with her partner from a position of strength. The children that she does have will tend to be healthier and better prepared. In addition, the improved health, education and earning capacity of women leads to better management of natural resources.

About half of the world's food is grown by women. It is estimated that two-thirds of women in developing countries work in agriculture, mostly in unpaid subsistence farming. They hoe, plant, weed, harvest, store the food, cook and take care of livestock. They walk miles and spend hours, sometimes days, collecting water, firewood and fodder. All this has provided women with profound knowledge about crop diversity, soil conditions and water quality. They are the ones who are most impacted by environmental degradation and have the most to gain by protecting the local ecosystems. Sustainable development begins and ends with women.

Speech prepared for the United Nations International Conference on Population and Development, Cairo, Egypt, September 7, 1994, when Fonda was goodwill ambassador for the United Nations Population Fund.

To give this a real voice, I'd like to quote a woman from Nepal whose words are in a pamphlet called "Seeds" that deals with forest conservation in Nepal: "By law, we villagers are only allowed to collect what has fallen on the ground in the forest. The trees are used for timber for building for those lucky enough to be sold a permit by the forest officers. Women are left with the leaves, branches and twigs. Once, it was too difficult to find wood on the ground, but now there is not even enough left over to fill one headload (about thirty-five pounds), unless you walk for miles and miles, and no fodder unless you cut the branches. Even when I travel a long way into the forest, I still have to cut branches illegally to get a large enough headload to cook for my family. If I'm caught by a forest guard, he takes my cutting tool, or tells me I have to pay a stiff fine, but what can I do? As it is now, I must bring my daughter with me to help collect fuel and fodder, so she often skips school to help me. I would rather that she got a good education so she would have a good chance in life, but I have no choice. There are too many other chores to complete. I now go to the forest every day that I have no work in the fields or grain to thresh or grind, and one headload lasts only a few days. If fuel gets even more scarce, I will have to take my daughter out of school completely so she can help me with my other tasks."

Evidence from numerous studies done in developing countries shows that when women are able to earn and control their money, they spend it in ways that benefit their families' health and welfare. Men, on the other hand, tend to spend their incomes on entertainment and consumer goods. In addition, women in developing countries deliver basic health care to their families and communities.

Given all this, why is it that women in these countries are discriminated against when it comes to education, inheritance, land ownership, jobs, training and resources? Why do girls receive less health care and food than boys? Why do women not fully participate in or benefit from development policies? Why is it that women are often not consulted when development programs are put into place? Over and over again, experience shows that when women are involved from the outset, programs stand a far better chance of succeeding and the lives and status of women and children are improved.

Too often, governments and lending institutions undermine women with poorly defined economic programs on the one hand, while at the same time trying to get them to limit fertility, wiping out with one program what is being attempted with another. There are numerous examples of development approaches in Africa and other parts of the world which give priority to men, even when women are the primary producers. For example, when cooperatives are formed, only one member of the family (which will turn out to be the male) is allowed to participate, freezing the women out of new input, training and access to land, making her subsistence work more difficult and increasing her need for more helping hands.

Another example is the large-scale agricultural intensification projects which put more demands on women's time and energy without compensation, reducing her ability to farm sustainably. Just as natural resources are not infinite, neither is women's energy. Both can only be stretched so far. By increasing women's need for children to help with the work, we also undermine women's desire to reduce child numbers. In some countries, Zimbabwe for example, there are active efforts to improve women's access to land and credit, modernize their livelihoods, and this is reflected not only in economic returns but in high contraceptive use.

Our approach to aid and development can be made more coherent if development plans, social and economic investment policies and national budgetary guidelines are reviewed at a high government level by some coordinating body in light of their fertility, as well as their justice, implications. Population policy cannot solely be in the purview of health ministries. Likewise, the policies of the international lending institutions should not compartmentalize population concerns, separating them from education, from promotion of livelihood, health and so forth. If population concerns are important, this concern should be spread throughout the development portfolio.

We mustn't permit our development policies to be driven by politics or special interests or even altruism, for that matter. They should be driven by enlightened self-interest. To quote Janice Jiggins in her book *Changing the Boundaries,* "Protecting and strengthening the capacities of girls and women is the bottom line in the survival of humankind as a species dependent on its environment. It is thus essential for human survival that economic theory, policy and practice in both rich and poor countries begins to measure, value and reward the services provided by women and by the environment."

The good news is that there is a slow but steadily growing appreciation that it makes economic, social and demographic sense to invest in women. This new direction is being led by innovative, smaller institutions such as Women's World Banking, ACCION International and Grameen Bank in Bangladesh, which have fostered women's economic entrepreneurship and independence.

Following their lead, larger bilateral and multilateral donors are beginning to direct more and more of their funds towards women. Why is this happening? Because the banks, always hard to impress, are impressed. They've seen that women can manage their finances well and that support for women's economic activities benefits the community at large and the health and education of the next generation. These lending institutions have begun to recognize that women in developing countries are agents of change.

We've begun to learn that, just as we can foster economic growth and fertility decline by investing in women, we can promote a more humane and equitable relationship between men and women which, as a by-product, encourages voluntary fertility decline. When a father shares the rearing of, and support for, his children, he may be more prone to share the mother's desire to limit family size. But there are countries where children still only have effective claims to their father's resources if the father wishes, or where the father's name appears on the birth certificate. There are countries in which the father's name only appears on the birth certificate if the parents are married. Even countries with "good laws" do not implement their ideal of shared parental responsibility. We must encourage men to be emotionally and financially responsible for their children. Let us hope that the young men of today grow up with a sense of responsibility about their sexuality, about their fertility and about parenting.

Can we afford to properly expand and improve our family planning programs world-wide? Can we afford to reproduce economic empowerment programs and education for women? You bet! In fact, we can't afford not to. It's a question of priorities and of developing a new understanding of national and global security. If the United States and the former Soviet Union could spend over $10 trillion during the Cold War to prepare for a possible threat, we can surely find enough money and resources to deal with dangers that are actually occurring.

We have to help create a critical mass for family planning and reducing consumption so that if a boy or girl is asked what they would do to help heal the world, they would start by saying, "I will live more simply and only have the number of children that I can support and care for." We need to communicate to people that life is sacred, that children have the right to be wanted and that it's irresponsible to have more children than you can support. But parents here in the developing countries, or in the North for that matter, cannot do this alone, individually. We must have commitments from our national governments to also invest in women and children and make them the center of our economic planning.

In a sense, we're asking ourselves to start doing what comes unnaturally. Throughout human history, we've been exhorted to go forth and multiply. All the Western religious doctrines have encouraged this. In part, it's because countries and churches needed bodies to fill the ranks of their armies as they went forth to fight the infidel. But it goes back even farther, hundreds of thousands of years to our ancestors, *Homo erectus.* At that time, evolutionary advantage went to those who were most adept at seeing and reacting to the most immediate danger, to those who spread their sperm wide and fast and early. On the other hand, *Homo erectus* who sat there pondering the implication of slaughtering all the woolly mammoths most likely had his head bitten off before he could reproduce. As the biologist E.O. Wilson said, "Prophets never enjoyed a Darwinian edge."

Our brains may not have evolved since those days, but reality has changed, and so must our thinking. We are not prisoners of our biology. We must reconceptualize the way we live in light of limited resources and a limited capacity to invest in the next generation. Quality, not quantity, is the path to the future.

All of us have important and difficult things to do. Change is always difficult and entails some discomfort and inconvenience. Population numbers are only part of the equation. The other part is what kind of consumers we are in the industrialized world and what kind of consumers we will become in the developing world.

We in the highly consuming countries must change our patterns of consumption, invest in the forgiving, energy-efficient, low-waste-producing technologies and share these technologies with the developing countries. We need to learn that enough is enough, that "more" doesn't necessarily translate into "happier."

People in the developing countries, with bilateral and multilateral support from aid-giving nations, must change their social investment patterns to support their women and children.

This is essentially what the Cairo Plan of Action is all about. It will require a shifting of gears, making some tough adjustments, but if we make them now, they can be humane and good, not especially jarring. If we don't, adjustments will be made for us by nature and they will be brutal and pitiless. If that occurs, we will not be the first species to have weakened and disappeared, nor the first civilization. History is littered with civilizations who fell victim to short-term definitions of self-interest. Let us learn from history.

THE NEW FEMINISM:
REUNITING THE HEAD, THE
HEART AND THE BODY

This has been an emotional three days. I don't think I'm the only one that has been filled with tears. They are tears of joy. When our bodies become tuning forks, vibrating with words spoken by sisters that enter us and hum with truth. Tears of realization not only that we are not alone, but that we are one. Tears of recognition that all of us are on a journey and none of us have arrived at a destination. It's not just me. It's all of us. Tears of relief to know that the path isn't supposed to be straight or easy or even. It's not just me that stumbles against obstacles. Gloria Steinem still does. Marion Woodman still does. And even Sister Joan Chittister does.

When my daughter read the brochure for this conference, she said, "Oh, Mom, it's so New Age. Yoga, meditation. Inner peace. I thought it was going to be political. The elections are two months away." Well, I understand her reaction. I would have had that reaction when I was thirty-five. Or forty-five. Or fifty-five.

I realized that if I was going to become an effective agent for change, I had some healing to do. And that things that we consider

Speech prepared for the Third Annual Women & Power Conference, Omega Institute, September 2004.

New Age, like music and dance and painting and drama therapy and prayer and laughter, can be part of the healing process. I know that it was while I was laughing when I first saw Eve Ensler perform *The Vagina Monologues* that my feminism slipped out of my head and took up residence in my body, where it has lived ever since. . . . embodied at last.

Up until then I had been a feminist in the sense that I supported women. I brought gender issues into my movie roles. I helped women make their bodies strong. I read all the books. I thought I had it in my heart and my body. I didn't. I didn't. I didn't. It was too scary. It was like stepping off a cliff without knowing if there was a trampoline down below to catch me. It meant rearranging my cellular structure. It meant doing life differently. And I was too scared. Women have internalized patriarchy's tokens in various ways but, for me, I silenced my true authentic voice all my life to keep a man. God forbid I should be without a man! Preferably an alpha male. Because without that, what would validate me?

And I needed to try to be perfect because I knew that if I wasn't, I would never be loved. As I sat on the panel yesterday, my sense of imperfection became focused on my body. I hated my body. It started around the beginning of adolescence. Before then I had been too busy climbing trees and wrestling with boys to worry about being perfect. What was more important than perfect was strong and brave. But then suddenly the wrestling became about sex and being popular and being right and good and perfect and fitting in. And then I became an actress in an image-focused profession. And, being competitive, I said, "Well, damn. If I'm supposed to be perfect, I'll show them." Which, of course, pitted me against other women and against myself. Carl Jung said perfection is for the gods. Completeness is what we mortals must strive for. Perfection is the curse of patriarchy. It makes us hate ourselves. And you can't be embodied if you hate your body. So one of the things we have to do is help our girls to get angry. Angry. Not at their own bodies, but at the paradigm that does this to us, to all of us. Let us usher perfection to the door and learn that good enough is good enough.

There's a theory of behavioral change called social inoculation. It means politicizing the problem. Let me tell you a story that explains this. In one of the ghettos of Chicago, young boys weren't going to school anymore. And community organizers found out they didn't have the "right" Nike Air Jordan shoes. So the organizers did something differently. They invited all the boys going to school into the community center and they took a Nike Air Jordan shoe and they dissected it. They cut off one layer of the rubber and they said, "See this? This is not a god. This was made in Korea. People were paid slave wages to make this, robbing your mothers and fathers of jobs." And he cut off another slice. And so it went. Deconstructing the Nike Air Jordan sneaker so the boys would understand the false god that they had been worshipping. We need to name the problem so that our girls can say, "It's not me and we're going to get mad."

We also have to stop looking over our shoulder to see who is the expert with the plan. We're the experts, if we allow ourselves to listen to what Marion Woodman calls our feminine consciousness. But this has been muted in a lot of us by the power-centered male belief center called patriarchy. I don't like that word. The first night Eve [Ensler] spoke about the old and new paradigm and never said the word. It's so rhetorical. It makes people's eyes glaze over. It did for me. The first time I ever heard Gloria Steinem use it back in the 1970s, I thought, "Oh, my God, what that means is men are bad and we have to replace patriarchy with matriarchy." Of course, given the way women are different than men, maybe a dose of matriarchy wouldn't be bad, maybe balancing things out. My favorite ex-husband, Ted Turner—maybe some of you saw him say it on Charlie Rose: "Men, we had our chance and we blew it—we have to turn it over to women now."

But I've come to see that it's not about replacing one -archy with another. It's about changing the social construct to one where power is not the chief operating principle.

There's this dual journey that we're on. There's the inner journey, this New Age stuff, and the outer journey. Let's talk about governments first. Governments normally work within the power paradigm and governments play a central role in making us who we are. An empathic government encourages a caring government. A government that operates from a "might makes right" place creates a nation of bullies, envied by the rest of the world for its things, but hated for its lack of goodness.

I first noticed this phenomenon of government when, many years ago, I was making a movie in a little town in Norway and there was a party scene. It was Ibsen's *A Doll House.* It took three days to shoot and I had a lot of chance to spend time with the local people and I kept thinking, "There's something very different about these people. It's—what can it be?" And as I began to talk to them, I realized it's because they felt seen by their government. They felt valued. They mattered. Pregnant women got free milk. There was maternity leave. All the things that make women's and men's lives easier was addressed by their government.

Michael Moore addresses this in *Bowling for Columbine.* He asks this very interesting question. The Canadians have the same TV shows and video games and more guns per capita than we do, but they're not violent. He interviews three or four teenagers in the parking lot of a fast-food restaurant. They look just like ours, tattooed and pierced and everything like that. But they don't lock their doors. And they said to him, "Of course health care is our birthright. And of course we are taken care of. By our government." And that's the difference.

I never told these stories in a context like this, but now I'm going to tell you two stories.

I went to Hanoi in 1972, in July. I was there while my government was bombing the country that had received me as a guest. I was in a lot of air raids. I was taken into a lot of air-raid shelters. Every time I would go into a shelter, the Vietnamese people would look at me and ask the interpreter—probably they thought I was Russian—who was this white woman? And when the interpreter would say American, they would get all excited and they would smile at me.

And I would search their eyes for anger. I wanted to see anger. It would have made it easier if I could have seen what I know would have been in *my* eyes if I were them. But I never did. Ever. One day I had been taken several hours south of Hanoi to visit what had been the textile capital of North Vietnam that was razed to the ground and we were in the car and suddenly the driver and my interpreter said, "Quick, get out!" All along the road there are these manholes that hold one person and you jump in them and you pull kind of a straw lid over to protect you from shrapnel if there's a raid. I was running down the street to get into one of these holes and suddenly I was grabbed from behind by a young girl. She was clearly a schoolgirl because she had a bunch of books tied with a rubber belt hanging over her shoulder and she grabbed me by the hand and ran with me in front of this peasant hut. And she pulled the straw thatch off the top of the hole and jumped in and pulled me in afterward. These are small holes. These are meant for one small Vietnamese person. She and I got in the hole and she pulled the lid over and the bombs started dropping and causing the ground to shake and I'm thinking, "This is not happening. I'm going to wake up. I'm not in a bomb hole with a Vietnamese girl whom I don't know." I could feel her breath on my cheek. I could feel her eyelash on my cheek. It was so small that we were crammed together.

Pretty soon the bombing stopped. It turned out it was not that close. She crawled out and I got out and I started to cry and I just said to her, "I'm so sorry. I'm so sorry. I'm so sorry." And she started to talk to me in Vietnamese. And the translator came over.

She must have been fourteen or fifteen. And she looked me straight in the eye and she said, "Don't be sorry for us. We know why we're fighting. It's you who don't know . . ."

Well, it couldn't have been staged. It was impossible for it to have been staged. This young girl says to me, "It's you—you have to cry for your own people because we know why we're fighting." And I'm thinking, "This must be a country of saints or something. Nobody gets angry."

Several days later I'm asked to go see a production of a play—a traveling troupe of Vietnamese actresses is performing. It's Arthur Miller's play *All My Sons.* They want me, as an American, to critique it to say if the capitalists are really the way they look. (Two-toned saddle shoes and a polka dot tie, and I was like, OK, that will work!) It's a story about a factory owner who makes parts for bombers during the Second World War. He finds out that his factory is making faulty parts for the bombers, which could cause an airplane crash, but he doesn't say anything because he doesn't want to lose his government contract. One of his sons is a pilot and dies in an airplane crash. The other son accuses a—attacks his father for putting greed and self-interest ahead of what was right. Well, I watched the play and I kept thinking, "Why are they doing this? There's a war going on. Why are they performing *All My Sons* in North Vietnam?" And I asked the director, "Why are you doing this?" And he said, "We are a small country. We cannot afford to hate you. We have to teach our people there are good Americans and there are bad Americans, so that they will not hate Americans because, one day when this war ends, we will have to be friends."

When you come back home from a thing like that and people talk about the enemy, you think, "Wait a minute. Will we ever have a government here that will go to such sophisticated lengths to help our people not hate a country that is bombing them?"

Anyway, this is what I mean by the role of a government. It wasn't an accident that people didn't look at me during a war with hatred in their eyes. Their government taught them to love and to separate good from evil. That, to me, is a lesson that I will never ever forget.

So there's a dual journey to be taken. There's an inner journey and an outer journey and there's no conceptual model for the vision that we're working for. There's no road map for the politics of love. It's never happened.

Women have never yet had a chance in all of history to make a revolution. But if we're going to lead, we have to become the change that we seek. We have to incubate it in our bodies and embody it. The teachers, healers and activists with the most impact are always people who embody their politics.

I'm going to tell you another story. I had been living in France for eight years from 1962 to 1970 and I decided to leave my—not my favorite ex-husband, but my first ex-husband—and come home to be an activist. And I realized that in order to do that properly, I had to get to know this country of mine again. And I decided that I was going to drive across the country for two months. It was during the spring of 1970. As I was driving, Nixon invaded Cambodia. Four students were killed at Kent State, two at Jackson State, 35,000 National Guard were called out in sixteen states and a third of the nation's campuses closed down. I was arrested five times. But when I think back over those difficult two months, none of that is what I remember.

I remember a woman who was on the staff of a GI coffeehouse in Texas near Fort Hood. Her name was Terry Davis. And the moment I was in her presence, I sensed something different. It wasn't something I had been missing because I didn't know it existed. But I felt different in her presence. Because she moved from a place of love. She saw me not as a movie star, but as a whole me that I didn't even know existed yet.

She was interested in why I had become an activist and what I was doing to get involved in the movement. We were planning an upcoming demonstration and she asked my opinion. And she included me in all the decisions to make sure I was comfortable. This was—this was very new for me. I was thirty-one years old. I had made *Barbarella*. I was famous. But this was new to me. I saw the same sensitivity and compassion in the way she dealt with the GIs from Fort Hood at the coffeehouse. Unlike others in the peace movement at that time, she didn't judge the young men who were on their way to Vietnam. She knew most of them were from poor rural or inner city situations and had no good alternatives.

It was my first time experiencing a woman's leadership and it was palpable, like sinking into a warm tub after a cold winter. It was also my first time experiencing someone who embodied her politics, who tried to model in her everyday life the sort of society that she was fighting for. She fought not only against the government that was waging the war and depriving soldiers of their basic rights, she also fought against the sexism, the power struggles and judgmentalism within the movement itself. During that difficult two-month trip, it was this time spent with Terry that stands out most deeply. A harbinger of the new world beyond -isms and -archy that I could envision because of her. She was in her power.

I chaired the campaign for adolescent pregnancy prevention, so I can't talk about power without talking about choice. You know, I used to wonder how is it that the so-called pro-lifers show so much concern for the fetus, the fertilized egg growing inside the woman, but so little concern for the woman herself. Or even for the child once it is born.

And then I realized it's because this whole issue has nothing to do with being pro-life or pro-fetus. It has everything to do with power and who has it.

Throughout history many of the most patriarchal regimes and institutions—Hitler, Pinochet, the Vatican, Bush—have been the most opposed to women controlling their reproduction. The life of the fetus is only the most recent strategy. In other countries at other times it's been national security, upholding the national culture. There have been many strategies.

But we have to understand reproduction and sexuality are keys to women's empowerment. Childbearing and child rearing are complex undertakings that can't be decided by a medical doctor or by policy makers or aging bishops—celibate on top of it.

Because that makes a woman an object. It dismisses her knowledge about her own body and her own life. And instead of enhancing her dignity and self-respect it belittles and disempowers her. Robbed of her reproductive health and contraceptive decision making, a woman loses an essential element of what it means to be human. We have to hold this reproductive choice as a basic human right.

I want to talk about men for a minute. I've been through three marriages now and I'm writing my memoirs, so I thought deeply about the marriages and my husbands and my father, and I feel it has made me love them even more because I have come to realize that patriarchy is toxic to men as well as women. We don't see it so clearly because in some ways it privileges them and it's kind of, "Well, men will be men. That's the way things are . . ." But it's why men split off from their emotions—why the empathy gene is plucked from their hearts. Why there's a bifurcation between their head and their heart.

The system that undermines the notion of masculinity, what it means to be a real man, is a poison that runs deep and crosses generations. Fathers learn the steps to the non-relational dance of patriarchy at their father's knees and their fathers probably learned it at the grandfather's knees. So the toxins continue generation after generation until now. We have to change the steps of the dance for ourselves and for our children.

Gloria Steinem said in one of her books that we need to change patriarchal institutions if we are to stop producing leaders whose lives are then played out on a national and international stage.

About four years ago I got to know Carol Gilligan. She is a feminist psychologist who transformed the landscape of psychology. It was like, "Oh, yeah. Women are left out. We better put them in." It's just fascinating.

What I learned, which helped me understand my own life a lot better and the lives of the girls that I work with, is that it's when girls reach puberty that the damage begins. Up until then we— you know, if you can remember, if you can think and remember how feisty you were before when you owned your voice. And then this thing happened and we lose it. And of course teaching our girls to maintain resistance and not go underground with it is critical. And it's so important for mothers to own our power because, I mean, I've had a very difficult relationship with my daughter and I know why. I'm like her rehearsal. I'm the one that's showing her what it's going to be like. And what did she see? She saw me giving away my power. Marriage after marriage after relationship. And she's been pissed all her life.

So it happens to us at twelve, thirteen, fourteen. But Carol Gilligan has three sons. She cares about boys. And she's researched boys. And she and her colleagues—you know what they discovered? The damage is done to boys around age five when they enter formal schooling. One out of ten young boys age five and six are on Ritalin in this country. It's when they—it's not even so much the parents are saying anything specific to them. They're entering the world and the message is, "Don't be a a sissy or a mama's boy. Forget your emotions." They become emotionally illiterate.

Understand what that means as activists. Of course girls are the agents of change. You don't have to scratch very deep for us to say that's damn right. Man, I remember when I was ten and it wasn't like that at all.

But for boys, it's always been that way. They can't remember a time when they weren't entitled, when they weren't supposed to be this way, you know. They're at a tremendous disadvantage. And we have to hold that in our hearts and especially those of us that have young sons or in my case grandson—my grandson is five and he just entered kindergarten and you don't think I'm vigilant? They need—they need this combination of complete unconditional love and a lot of structure. But they have to be witnessed. They have to be seen. Some adult has to be present for them. And talking about the heart and about emotions to allow our young boys to come up and be worthy of our daughters.

I'm fascinated by the link between control of nature and control of women. It's very old, you know. Back in the fifteenth and sixteenth centuries, women were put on a rack or burned because they were different. At that same time, Francis Bacon, who is called the father of reason—he's the one who came up with knowledge is power, that was his line—he said that we must put nature on the rack. Interesting. They were doing it to women and to nature.

I read, in the Gnostic gospels, a new version of the Garden of Eden myth and it was an epiphany for me. (When I first read this version of the Garden of Eden I felt like someone had said "welcome home.") God looks down—God looks down and sees Adam: man. And he says something is missing. All atoms and molecules are there and everything, but there's no consciousness. And so he sends down Eve, life, consciousness. The feminine spirit, light. She is dropped down and quickens the body of Adam into what today is our unique species. We are the only species who can observe the universe. We can be observers. I always wondered how come. Why? It's the feminine spirit. We didn't cause the downfall of man. We weren't an afterthought. We quickened him into being.

Saying Eve caused the downfall has robbed us of this—cut us off from our life source, from our Eve. God intended for there to be a balance.

That's why there's no -archy. A balance between man, strength, balance, assertiveness—very important things to have—and a woman, fluid in the present, connected to earth, intuitive, chaotic. Every human being has both of those. We live in a matrix that combines those elements. The danger is when it gets out of kilter and the masculine rises to the detriment of the feminine in an individual or in a nation or in the world. When that happens, there is war, lust, power, denigration of what's sacred. So our task is to bring back the balance. In ourselves, in our families, our communities, and in the world.

It's so hard because patriarchy has been around so long that we just think that's life. It's ordained. An argument can be made that there was a time in history when it was necessary to build civilizations out of societies that were hunter-gatherers. Somebody has to be in charge.

But you can also make an argument that that paradigm has outlived its usefulness and is destroying everything. It's destroying balance. It's destroying nature. It's destroying men. It's destroying women. So our task is to bring back balance. Our task is to elect the least patriarchal guy.

I vote for the one that says that terrorism has to be dealt with, with sensitivity. And you know why? Because it's true. You have to understand why young men want to blow themselves up. What is the cause of it? Before the conference began, we were talking about this issue and of how Dick Cheney made fun of John Kerry because he said we have to be sensitive. But someone said, "You know, suppose we had a president that would actually get Osama and say, 'Let's talk.' " And she used the example of Gorbachev and Reagan when the arms race was turned around and someone asked Gorbachev, "What happened between you and Reagan?"

And Gorbachev said, "We talked." Talking. There's a chemical change that happens when people really show up for each other. Imagine what would happen if we just sat down with Osama and said, "Okay. Now, tell me what's the problem?" And we really—it would be totally disarming, you know. It would be great.

You have to see a movie called *What the Bleep Do I Know!?* It's about quantum physics, Judeo–Christian theories and change. One character in the movie is played by Marlee Matlin, the wonderful deaf actress. She's in a subway and sees these huge vials of water with photographs over them. The first one explains that the vial of water was taken from a large body of water in Japan and the cells were photographed through a microscope, just randomly. The second photograph was taken of the water cells when they had been blessed by a Buddhist monk. They were like snowflakes. They had reformed themselves into these beautiful structures because they had been blessed. And then there was another photograph of the cells where overnight the words "I love you" had been taped to the water and again, they were beautiful. They had changed again into these wonderful shapes. And then there was another one where the words had been taped "I hate you. I want to kill you." And the cells looked like knives. They were jagged and they were ugly and they were dangerous. Then this man comes up to her and says, "It makes you think, doesn't it?" You know, if a thought can do that to the cells of water, think what it can do to you.

What this says is that change is mysterious and we must not lose hope. That's why this conference is so important. If we can communicate through our hearts and souls and bodies what has happened to us today, that cellular change that has taken place—do you feel it? Yeah. If you can transfer that to the people you're going back to, we're going to become a tipping point. You know, what we're seeing now is the balance so out of kilter, so barnacled with the wrong kind of power and lust. But think about what happens to a wounded beast. It's always right before the beast dies that it becomes the most dangerous. And it thrashes and flails. But most of us who have been here today know that right beneath the surface, a great tectonic shift is taking place.

I'll tell you why I know it. Have you ever been to Yellowstone National Park? Yellowstone is the place in the world next to Siberia where the earth's crust is the most thin. Where the molten interior of the earth pops out. Old Faithful is the most well-known example of this. But if you walk through the park you can see steam rising above the trees and over here mud bubbling up from cracks and crevices in the crust.

I've traveled all over the world. Sometimes with Eve Ensler. Sometimes on my own. But I've seen the steam. And I've seen the mud bubbling up. And it's women and men all over the world that are starting to come through those cracks and crevices. It's an army of love and that's what we have to be. We have to ripen the time and turn that steam and those bubbles into a volcano. So let's be a volcano. Thank you. Thank you very much. We're going to end this in prayer. We want to go out on a prayerful note.

FEMALE EMPOWERMENT AND THE BATTLE OVER REPRODUCTIVE RIGHTS

I used to puzzle over why the people who want to outlaw abortion are the same people who want to do away with sexuality education and contraceptives, the very things which would help make abortion unnecessary.

Then I came to realize that this whole issue has nothing to do with "the life of the fetus," that, at least for the real anti-choice activists, the fetus has nothing to do with it. Have you ever asked yourself why these activists show so much concern for the fertilized egg growing inside the woman but so little concern for the child once it is actually born? Take a look at the states with strict anti-abortion laws and how much money they devote to children's programs such as aid to needy children, pre- and post-natal care, etc., and compare their child-related spending with states which have the least restrictive laws.

Louisiana, for example, with the nation's most stringent anti-abortion laws, spends an average of $602 per child. Hawaii, on the other hand, with the least restrictive abortion laws, spends $4,648. It would seem that for those who oppose abortion, life begins with conception and ends at birth.

Speech prepared for the 2000 Utahns for Choice Annual Dinner.

Opposing choice and opposing contraception has nothing to do with pro-life or pro-fetus; it has everything to do with power and who has it. Reproduction and sexuality are keys to women's empowerment. If a woman is able to determine the reproductive and sexual aspects of her life, it means she can also control and determine many others aspects of her life.

This power struggle has existed from the very beginning of the 120-year struggle over reproductive rights. Those who would oppose women's self-determination in the reproductive arena have used different strategies along the way. Granting personhood to the fetus is only the last incarnation in a long line of strategies beginning with the 1873 Comstock Act that was a reaction to the beginnings of the modern United States women's movement.

The Comstock Act was backed by the Young Men's Christian Association and the powerful industrialists who sat on this board. It led a crusade to "sanitize" America society by ridding it of any and every work, representation, or object deemed to be "obscene, lewd, or lascivious." It was primarily aimed at "any article or thing designed or intended for the prevention of contraception or procuring abortion." The legal argument under which contraception and contraceptive information were criminalized was "obscenity." The dissemination of contraceptives and information about contraceptives were also criminalized.

An anti-abortion tract of the time put it this way: "Sexual intercourse, unhallowed by the creation of a child, is lust. . . . Wife without children is mere sewer to pass off the unfruitful and degraded passions and lusts of one man."

During this time, the battle against contraception and abortion was joined by a new set of allies—the medical profession. Up until then, care during pregnancy and childbirth was the domain of women: female midwives, and lay healers. But professional physicians lobbied for legislation that would enable them to assert their authority over health care through a state licensing system that would exclude those not trained in professional schools. Most specifically, and to the detriment of women in the areas of obstetrics and gynecology, the doctors were attempting to bring pregnancy and childbirth into their exclusive domain.

Oftentimes, allegations about links between health and morality were absolutely flagrant. For example, a Boston gynecologist said that condoms degraded love and caused lesions and that the lesions were "God's little allies in promoting chastity"—sound familiar in this age of HIV and AIDS?

In 1871, the American Medical Association's committee on criminal abortion wrote this of the woman who has had an abortion: "She becomes unmindful of the course marked out for her by providence, she overlooks the duties imposed on her by the marriage contract. She yields to the pleasures—but shrinks from the pains and responsibilities of maternity; and, destitute of all delicacy and refinements, resigns herself, body and soul, into the hands of unscrupulous and wicked men. . . . She sinks into an old age like a withered tree, stripped of its foliage; with the stain of blood upon her soul she dies without the hand of affection to smooth her pillow."

Around 1918, following the trial of Margaret Sanger, an exception was made to the obscenity law so that dispensing contraceptives for medical purposes by a licensed physician fell outside prohibition laws. In other words, contraceptives became legal, but only if channeled through the special expertise of licensed physicians.

Of course, for the anti-abortion forces, the advent of the pill in the 1960s was tantamount to Armageddon. In a new book by Lionel Tiger called *The Decline of Males,* he argues that males are in decline largely due to female-controlled contraception: "It is impossible to over-estimate the importance of the contraceptive pill on human arrangements." By making promiscuity less risky, the pill allows sex for sex's sake and, more importantly, allows women to control reproduction. Tiger believes that women's power over contraception alienates men from the means of reproduction, creating what he calls "paternity uncertainty."

This is a mind-set that values women mainly for their services as wives and sexual partners to men and as producers and rearers of children. This view does not reflect reality. Virtually everywhere in the world women are active and indispensable participants in both the formal and informal labor markets, in agriculture, small businesses, the service sector, and in the industrialized world as corporate executives. It reflects a mind-set that believes that women cannot be trusted to make decisions that will be good for their families and society; that what is good for a family and a community and a society or even a woman's own health is something that must be determined by others who "know better" and then imposed on her.

Robbed of reproductive health and contraceptive decision making, a woman loses an essential element of what it means to be a full human being.

FIGHTING
MARGARET SANGER'S BATTLE

On March 29, 2003, Planned Parenthood Federation of America, at its Salute to Courage, Integrity, and Leadership conference, presented Jane Fonda with the Margaret Sanger Award. The federation cited Fonda as "a passionate advocate for reproductive rights and a leader in the field of teen pregnancy prevention."

Do we need to ask if Margaret Sanger is rolling over in her grave? I wonder if she's surprised that we're still fighting this battle. I bet she's not surprised and we shouldn't be either. This is the mother of all battles. This will be the last battle. Why? Opposing choice and opposing contraception has nothing to do with pro-life or pro-fetus; it has everything to do with power and who has it.

This is a battle that has existed for over 120 years. Those who would oppose women's self-determination in the reproductive arena have used different strategies along the way. Granting personhood to the fetus is only the latest incarnation.

It started with the Comstock Act in 1873 that outlawed any discussion of contraception on the grounds it was lewd and obscene. After Margaret Sanger's trial in 1918, contraceptives for

Speech prepared for Planned Parenthood Honors: A Salute to Courage, Integrity, and Leadership gala, Portland, Oregon, March 29, 2003.

medical purposes could only be given out by licensed physicians. By then, women's reproductive health had been taken out of the hands of the women—who had traditionally done the work like midwives (they still can't be licensed in Georgia)—and put into the hands of male doctors, many of whom didn't approve of women using contraceptives.

Other countries have used other strategies. For instance, in Algeria contraception and abortion were once viewed as an attack on Algerian culture and its view of women's role as exclusively wives and mothers. In the Chile of General Pinochet, reproductive rights were viewed as a threat to national security.

Reproductive health has to be understood from a woman's point of view. Okay, there are some women who oppose choice—I call them ventriloquists for the patriarchy—but we must not forget that a woman manages her fertility through a spectrum of factors that include her relations, sexual and otherwise, with her partner; her economic and psychological circumstances; her status within the family and in the community; and her future security. Health factors are only one among all these others. Childbearing and child rearing are a complex undertaking that affects a woman's economic, social, sexual, and emotional life and the life of her family and her community. This undertaking cannot be decided by a medical doctor who is weighing it from the point of view of health risks, or of policy makers who may view it subjectively as a moral issue. This makes the woman an "object" and it dismisses her knowledge about her own body and her own life. Instead of enhancing her dignity and self-respect, it belittles and disempowers her.

So . . . onward Planned Parenthood of America!

Your strategies are right on target: mega-organizing, social marketing and business strategies. We have to change the political and social climate for reproductive rights and sexual health.

Let's all do our part. And thank you again!

AGAINST THE REALISTS

I didn't want to do this—be on a stage in the middle of a room talking to people I can't see, not even for V-Day and the grand vision it represents. I get paralyzed with stage fright. I did it at Madison Square Garden last year and for the prior week, I prayed to be hit by a car—not killed or anything, just maimed a little, enough to be sent to a hospital till the event was over.

But then, two days ago, I read the article in the *New York Times Magazine* about Eve Ensler and it made me mad—that brand of snide, journalistic cynicism that seems to be reserved for females of the species who represent hope and inspiration, especially if they have an abundance of energy, especially if they hold a grand vision. Visions, you see, are very suspect for those who still cling to the old, rule-of-the-fathers way of seeing things. "How dare she have a grand vision! How dare she dream of something that seems to me very unrealistic!"

The journalist is commenting on Eve's plan to end violence against women. She feels alienated by it and asks, "Where's the plan of action?" And I wondered if the writer had ever attended the World Economic Forum. Usually it meets in Davos, Switzerland. August body it is—all the world's great economists and leaders, the

Speech prepared for the V-Day fund-raiser to stop violence against women and girls, New York City, February 16, 2002.

men who run things! I was there once, permitted in because I was married to Ted Turner. It was a few years ago, just after the collapse of the Asian markets.

I was there in the room and I watched carefully. You know what I learned? They don't have a plan, these men in whose hands rest our newly globalized economies. They don't quite know where they're going. I wonder if the *New York Times* journalist would have noticed and felt alienated—probably not—not when it's them, the "realists."

I read this *New York Times* article just as I was finishing a book by poet and writer Robin Morgan called *Demon Lover: On the Sexuality of Terrorism.* In the last chapter she writes a sort of personal meditation about the nature of transformation from the compartmentalized, hierarchical, ejaculatory, androcentric power structure to a politics of Eros, a politics of love—a process of transformation that passes under the radar of world economists and cynical journalists.

I want to read excerpts from that chapter. While I do, think about the 800 performances of *The Vagina Monologues* that are being performed around the world, the many hundreds that have alreacy been performed, and imagine the thousands and thousands of women who are coming to witness and speak—women who have never before broken the silence and spoken in the presence of othcr women about their experiences of violence or thc pleasures of their bodies, women who now know they are not alone.

Robin Morgan writes, "Silence is the first thing within the power of the enslaved to shatter. From that shattering, everything else spills forth." Shatter the silence and everything else spills forth. Now, think about the flocking of tens of thousands of starlings and the schools of fish that turn instantly, on a dime, in a flash, all together, as though choreographed. Scientists can't explain the phenomenon. There is no plan of action. No individual is a leader, or in another sense, every individual is.

And think about chaos theory, which posits that an imperceptible and implicit order is at work beneath a seeming disorder. Change is mysterious.

In the chapter I'm quoting from, Robin Morgan writes in the third person, of herself, of all women, of me, on a journey of transformation to the new politics. Robin, if you're here, forgive me for taking some liberties:

She begins to love herself, to love her own flesh, to love her own genius. She begins to deserve herself—this is political—this is the discovery of ecstasy, not as "standing outside" the self but as standing, for the first time, *inside* the self. She begins to imagine what she deserves from others. She begins to imagine what others deserve. She listens carefully for all hints of audacity. She watches, learns, and tries to adopt the unpredictable organic strategies of other women.

She learns about village mountain women in the Himalayas, who've organized to preserve the environment and to make themselves self-sufficient. They see these two issues as one because the average woman in this extremely poor region (where there is one gynecologist for every 300,000 women) spends over four hours a day gathering firewood and fetching water.

The women began mobilizing in 1974, when twenty-four of them started to embrace trees to protect them from commercial logging. This was the origin of the Chipko, the "embrace" movement. The government sent in troops to shoot anyone hugging trees. The women clung to the trees and the troops were too ashamed to fire. So the government and the loggers sent in elephants to trample the women who were draping themselves around the trees. The huge animals moved forward on command. The women left the trees and approached the elephants, singing a ritual song that Hindu women sing at the annual festival of the elephant god, when they bedeck temple elephants with garlands. But these were not temple elephants, they were army elephants.

Still, the women approached, singing, and then they swarmed over the animals, stroking them, embracing the massive trunks and feet. Was this a tactic or a prayer? Did the women believe in an elephant god? Or did they act in this manner simply because retreat was unthinkable and they saw no other option? No one knows and the women will not say.

But the elephants stopped. The elephants knelt. The elephants would not budge. The troops and loggers withdrew, acknowledging defeat before a group of women who were hugging trees.

In her growing epistemology, Robin Morgan finds Chipko an example of the politics of Eros and she learns of many other instances of female energy and audacity, in Greece, Brazil, Ireland, Israel, Nigeria.

But, she frets to herself, what effect are these women really having? They have no plan, they don't fully know what they're doing. Then she thinks, the men claim *they* have a plan—what effect are they really having?

Oppression, she suddenly realizes, always structures itself along the same monotonous pattern. Oppression is predictable. What *we* are, she sees, is *unpredictable.* Like freedom. And what we must dare become is *more* unpredictable.

She comprehends—it is not merely the absence of war but the presence of peace, not merely the absence of tragedy but the presence of comedy, not merely the absence of hate but the presence of love. And it is not merely the absence of fear but the presence of trust.

She comprehends that she is leaving no one behind, because it is not about the absence of men but about the presence of women.

Here in her own centrality, she sees to her astonishment that *he* is awkwardly, slowly, being drawn to her magnetism, methods, imaginings, desires. He stumbles, lurches, still brings others down with him when he falls. But a few of him begin to take, as she did, small incremental steps . . . truly caring for a child, trying to study peace, moving to the place her job requires, not merely "helping her with the housework," but voting for her, listening to her, trying to talk about this politics with other men, trying to make the connections.

The irony is that for the first time in her collective memory she has done nothing for the sake of drawing him; it is the side effect. She is the issue, she and these women. This is the new humanity, in which she feels for the first time fully human. What he is drawn to is her energy, an energy that is squared (or circled?) as she connects with other women.

Seemingly leaderless, these groups of women actually pass different kinds of leadership among themselves, varying their strengths as the situation requires. They speak myriad languages but they converse in female. They help one another to grieve, they teach one another to laugh, they excite one another to survive, they arouse one another to act. They recognize each other. They recognize that each other exists.

There are no models for this. The leaders have mapped no terrain beyond the revolutions of their own racking wheel.

Yet this terrain is authentic. She is experiencing it in all her senses, hungrily, rapidly, as if she were giving birth to herself as a new life form, as if she were being welcomed into the planet by the planet itself.

And Robin Morgan also says, "This I know: unless the majority of the human species which women constitute—the majority that has lived daily and nightly under a terrorism so ancient and omnipresent as to be called civilization—unless that enormous body of ordinary experiential experts address and engage this issue, it can never be understood, much less solved."

MY THIRD ACT

Before I turned sixty I thought I was a feminist. I was in a way—I worked to register women to vote, I supported women getting elected. I brought gender issues into my movie roles, I encouraged women to get strong and healthy, I read the books we've all read. I had it in my head and partly in my heart, yet I didn't fully get it.

See, although I've always been financially independent, and professionally and socially successful, behind the closed doors of my personal life I was still turning myself into a pretzel so I'd be loved by an alpha male. I thought if I didn't become whatever he wanted me to be, I'd be alone, and then I wouldn't exist.

There is not the time nor the place to explain why this was true, or why it is such a common theme for so many otherwise strong, independent women. Nor is it the time to tell you how I got over it (I'm writing my memoirs, and all will be revealed). What's important is that I did get over it. Early on in my third act I found my voice and, in the process, I have ended up alone . . . but not really. You see, I'm with myself and this has enabled me to see feminism more clearly. It's hard to see clearly when you're a pretzel.

So I want to tell you briefly some of what I have learned in this

Speech given at National Women's Leadership Summit, Washington, D.C., June 12, 2003.

first part of my third act and how it relates to what, I think, needs to happen in terms of a revolution.

Because we can't just talk about women being at the table—it's too late for that—we have to think in terms of the shape of the table. Is it hierarchical or circular (metaphorically speaking)?

We have to think about the quality of the men who are with us at the table, the culture that is hovering over the table that governs how things are decided and in whose interests. This is not just about glass ceilings or politics as usual. This is about revolution. I have finally gotten to where I can say that word and know what I mean by it and feel good about it because I see, now, how the future of the earth and everything on it, including men and boys, depends on this happening.

Let me say something about men: obviously, I've had to do a lot of thinking about men, especially the ones who've been important in my life, and what I've come to realize is how damaging patriarchy has been for them. And all of them are smart, good men who want to be considered the "good guys." But the Male Belief System, that compartmentalized, hierarchical, ejaculatory, androcentric power structure that is patriarchy, is fatal to the hearts of men, to empathy and relationship.

Yes, men and boys receive privilege and status from patriarchy, but it is a poisoned privilege for which they pay a heavy price. If traditional, patriarchal socialization takes aim at girls' voices, it takes aim at boys' hearts—makes them lose the deepest, most sensitive and empathic parts of themselves. Men aren't even allowed to be depressed, which is why they engage so often in various forms of self-numbing, from sex to alcohol and drugs to gambling and workaholism. Patriarchy strikes a Faustian bargain with men.

Patriarchy sustains itself by breaking relationship. I'm referring here to real relationship, the showing-up kind, not the "I'll stay with him 'cause he pays the bills, or because of the kids, or because if I don't I will cease to exist," but relationship where you, the woman, can acknowledge your partner's needs while simultaneously acknowledging and tending to your own. I work with young girls and I can tell you there's a whole generation who have not learned what a relationship is supposed to feel like—that it's not about leaving themselves behind.

Now, every group that's been oppressed has its share of Uncle Toms, and we have our Aunt Toms. I call them ventriloquists for the patriarchy. I won't name names but we all know them. They are women in whom the toxic aspects of masculinity hold sway. It should neither surprise nor discourage us. We need to understand it and be able to explain it to others, but it means, I think, that we should not be just about getting a woman into this position, or that. We need to look at "Is that woman intact emotionally? Has she had to forfeit her empathy gene somewhere along the way for whatever reason?"

And then, of course, there are what Eve Ensler calls vagina-friendly men, who choose to remain emotionally literate. It's not easy for them—look at the names they get called: wimp, pansy, pussy, soft, limp, momma's boy. Men don't like to be considered "soft" on anything, which is why more don't choose to join us in the circle. Actually, most don't have the choice to make. You know why? Because, when they are little (I learned this from Carol Gilligan), like five years or younger, boys internalize the message of what it takes to be a "real man." Sometimes it comes through their fathers who beat it into them. Sometimes it comes because no one around them knows how to connect with their emotions. Sometimes it comes because our culture rips boys from their mothers before they are developmentally ready. Sometimes it comes because boys are teased at school for crying. It can be a specific trauma that shuts them down. But, I can assure you, it is true to some extent of many, if not most, men and when the extreme version of it manifests itself in our nation's leaders, beware!

Another thing that I've learned is that there is a fundamental contradiction not just between patriarchy and relationship, but between patriarchy and democracy. Patriarchy masquerades as democracy, but it's an anathema. How can it be democracy when someone has to always be above someone else, when women, who are a majority, live within a social construct that discriminates against them, keeps them from having their full human rights?

Maybe at some earlier stage in human evolution, patriarchy was what was needed just for the species to survive. But today, there's nothing threatening the human species but humans. We've conquered our predators, we've subdued nature almost to extinction, and there are no more frontiers to conquer or to escape into so as to avoid having to deal with the mess we've left behind. Frontiers have always given capitalism, patriarchy's economic face, a way to avoid dealing with its shortcomings. Well, we're having to face them now in this post-frontier era and inevitably—especially when we have leaders who suffer from toxic masculinity—that leads to war, the conquering of new markets, and the destruction of the earth.

However, it is altogether possible that we are on the verge of a tectonic shift in paradigms—that what we are seeing happening today are the paroxysms, the final terrible death throes of the old, no longer workable, no longer justifiable system. Look at it this way: it's patriarchy's third act and we have to make sure it is its last.

It's possible that the extreme, neoconservative version of patriarchy which makes up our current executive branch will overplay its hand and cause the house of cards to collapse. We know that this new "preventive war" doctrine will put us on a permanent war footing. We know there can't be guns and butter, right? We learned that with Vietnam. We know that a Pandora's box has been opened in the Middle East and that the administration is not prepared for the complexities that are emerging. We know that friends are becoming foes and angry young Muslims with no connection to al-Qaeda are becoming terrorists in greater numbers. We know that with the new tax plan the rich will be better off and the rest will be poorer. We know what happens when poor young men and women can only get jobs by joining the military and what happens when they come home and discover that the day after Congress passed the "Support Our Troops" resolution, $25 billion was cut from the Veterans Administration budget. We know that already, families of servicemen have to go on welfare and are angry about it.

So, as Eve Ensler says, we have to change the verbs from *obliterate, dominate, humiliate,* to *liberate, appreciate, celebrate.* We have to make sure that head and heart can be reunited in the body politic, and relationship and democracy can be restored.

We need to really understand the depth and breadth of what a shift to a new, feminine paradigm would mean, how fundamentally central it is to every single other thing in the world. We win, everything wins, including boys, men, and the earth. We have to really understand this and be able to make it concrete for others so they will be able to see what feminism really is and see themselves in it.

So, our challenge is to commit ourselves to creating the tipping point and the turning point. The time is ripe to launch a unified national movement, a campaign, a tidal wave, built around issues and values, not candidates.

That's why V-Day, the White House Project and their many allies, are partnering to hold a national women's convention somewhere in the heartland, next June of 2004. Its purpose will be to inspire and mobilize women and vagina-friendly men around the 2004 elections and to build a new movement that will coalesce our energies and forces around a politics of caring.

The convention will put forward a fresh, clear, and concise platform of issues, and build the spirit, energy and power base to hold the candidates accountable for them. There will be a diversity of women from across the country who will participate in the mobilization. There will be a special focus on involving young women.

There will be a variety of performers and artists acknowledging that culture plays a powerful role in political action. There will be a concurrent Internet mobilization. Women's organizations will be asked to sign on and send representatives to the convention.

There will be a caravan, a rolling tour across the country, of diverse women leaders, celebrities and activists who will work with local organizers to build momentum, sign people up, register them to vote, get them organized and leave behind a tool kit for further mobilization through the election and beyond.

This movement will be a volcano that will erupt in a flow of soft, hot, empathic, breathing, authentic, vagina-friendly, relational lava that will encircle patriarchy and smother it. We will be the flood and we'll be Noah's ark. *V* for Vagina, for vote, for victory.

WOMEN AND MEN AND THE HEAD/HEART BUSINESS

I've spent a lot of time thinking about this head/heart business in relation to the men in my life: specifically my three husbands and my father. All good men, none deliberately cruel or mean, but all with a disconnect between head and heart. And all of them have *suffered* from this disconnect and they numbed the pain of this in various ways including alcohol, sex, gambling, never being still. My dad was a little different. He managed to create safety valves through which he could express the other parts of himself, the heart parts, if you will: through acting, painting, needlepoint, macrame and gardening, all more or less solitary occupations that didn't require him to *relate* to anyone.

All these men loved me, I think, but they didn't know how to *join* me. And I was their accomplice in this because I never let them really know me. I learned early on, in those proverbial times when children learn everything, that to be loved, a girl has to be perfect. Oh, I was a rebellious girl, and when I grew up, I was a strong, independent woman professionally, politically, financially, even, but behind the closed doors of my most intimate relations, I could turn myself into a pretzel to be whatever the man wanted me to be be-

Speech prepared for Smart Talk Women's Lecture Series, Hotel Dupont, Wilmington, Delaware, March 31, 2004.

cause otherwise, how could he love me? I was really good at it. Trust me, my Academy Awards should be for my private life.

And what was I doing? I was creating the same bifurcation between my head and my heart that the men suffered from and I didn't even know it. I was forfeiting relationship with myself in order to be in relationship with a man.

Being with a man, an alpha man, in particular, was so important that I was willing to leave myself behind—which wasn't so difficult since I didn't know who "myself" was.

Up until that sixtieth birthday, I was a feminist in the sense that I supported women, I brought gender issues into my movie roles, helped women make their bodies strong, I read all the books. I had it in my head. I thought I had it in my heart, but I didn't. Not where it really counts. It was too scary; it was like stepping off a cliff without knowing if there was a trampoline down below. I had to build my foundation first and it turned out that, by preparing for my sixtieth, by going all the way back to the beginning and *feeling* my way forward—it was like Hansel and Gretel's path of breadcrumbs leading me along—that is when I was really helped by what Gloria Steinem has written about how we women leave behind the girl we were, strong and feisty, in order to become the "good" woman we're "supposed to be" and when we get older, if we are lucky and work at it, how we can circle back to that feisty girl and know her again for the first time.

Right after the breakup of my last marriage I reread Carol Gilligan's *In a Different Voice,* which Gloria Steinem had given me years before when my second marriage had broken up. Timing is everything. I wasn't ready then. From Carol's book, I learned how the Male Role Belief System, that compartmentalized, hierarchical, ejaculatory, androcentric power structure that is patriarchy, is anathema to relationship. Patriarchy *sustains* itself and *repeats* itself by breaking relationships. It *depends* on the bifurcation of head and heart for its very existence and we tend to see this as "just the way things are—that's life." "The essence of human development is that psychological growth takes place in relationship. Relationship brings the oxygen of experience into the psyche."

What I've discovered over the last four or five years as I try to understand my marriages (and my father) and the head/heart thing is how damaging patriarchy is, not just to women and girls, but to men and boys. I am glad that I really understand now in the most personal ways, why a feminist revolution will be good for men and boys. I am not talking about switching to a matriarchy and replacing one form of hierarchy with another. No, men have to make this journey with us. But it's harder for them.

You see, while being "male" and "female" is innate, "masculinity" and "femininity" are not. They're not states of being; they're acquired social constructs. Masculinity is conferred, the way you confer membership in an exclusive club, and membership can always be revoked—men have to constantly prove, over and over again, through achievement (or, failing that, through violence), through being *above* someone else, that you are deserving of membership. How exhausting!

I think it was in Susan Faludi's book *Backlash* where I read about an opinion poll that had been taken asking men and women around the world how they defined "masculinity." The overwhelming response was "the ability to bring home the bacon, to support their family." So, if this is the main criteria for membership in the "masculinity club" everywhere in the world, what happens when unemployment among men goes up while women (albeit at lower wages and no benefits) have jobs? Violence against women is what goes up . . . right? That's the other big criteria for proving manhood, for membership in the club. You're no wimp, you're tough, someone's below you who you can beat up on.

And guess what, there's a new paradigm bubbling just beneath the surface ready to replace the old. People are calling it many different names: the Feminine, the Good Mother, the Politics of Caring. Call it what you will, it represents a changing of all the most fundamental precepts that have governed civilization for the last 10,000 years, so that head and heart can be reunited and relationship and democracy restored. To me, this is what feminism means and it includes men . . . those men whose heads and hearts are united. All of us contain both masculine and feminine, but if the masculine aspect becomes overly predominant in its bifurcated, out-of-touch-with-feelings aggressiveness, that is when we are in trouble. If the men and women in whom these toxic traits are dominant also happen to be in leadership positions, then something decisive and immediate needs to happen to rectify things and bring back the balance.

I think it is up to women and girls to lead the way. I'd like to tell you a couple of stories that have shown me why this is true. Sometimes we can see things more clearly when we go outside of our own familiar context.

Several years ago, I traveled to Nigeria with the International Women's Health Coalition to make a documentary on three girls' programs which were started by Nigerian feminists in Nigeria. All three of these women had previously been part of a national organization called WIN—Women in Nigeria. After ten years of what had appeared on the surface to be a successful effort, these brave women decided to evaluate WIN's work.

They learned that although Nigerian women had flocked to WIN's workshops and conventions, they didn't bring their newly acquired skills and consciousness home with them. Again, behind the closed doors of their intimate relationship, their newly acquired voice would go silent.

Faced with this discovery, the Nigerian women organizers decided they should change strategies and concentrate their efforts on the daughters, *before* they had internalized oppression the way their mothers had. And I can tell you, it is working—which is incredibly profound and important given that Nigeria is one of the

most conservative countries in Africa. Each program takes a different approach as befits the local culture. In the more liberal south,
they focus unapologetically, smack dab, on gender empowerment,
helping girls understand why they have the right to safety, to say
no, to control their bodies. In Lagos, the capital, in the middle part
of Nigeria, the program focuses on reproductive rights and sexuality and includes boys. In the conservative, Muslim north, they
focus on micro-enterprise, teaching poor women to type and sew.
In all three places, girls (and vagina-friendly boys) are claiming
their power. And what I learned there was that when girls get
strong and connected with themselves, boys are forced to deal with
it, to test their own capacity for emotion and authenticity. It starts
sometimes with the boys pretending they're feminists just to get
these newly empowered girls to date them—because, of course,
they are the most interesting girls! But, you know, if you pretend
long enough you start to become.

Research over the last three or four decades has revealed the developmental underpinnings of *why* girls and women are the agents
of change. Let me try to sum it up: boys lose their relational voice
early in their development, as I just mentioned, usually around five
years old, the time when they enter formal schooling. Boys become invested so early in the definition of masculinity as "man
being entitled; man being superior to woman, man being superior
to boys and other men." It's "just the way things are," it's ordained.

Girls, on the other hand, have a good decade or more of experiencing their voice before they feel the pressure to become silent,
which generally happens at the cusp of puberty when we are told
what the criteria is to enter the "Femininity Club" and be "good
girls," selfless, not too smart, not too loud, not too strong or uppity.

For girls, then, "fitting in," capitulating to cultural norms, is a
learned experience. They *remember* the "before" part of it—we don't
need to scratch too deeply to get at it and release their righteous
anger and raise their resistance. It's much harder with boys; we

need to get to them much earlier and offer attractive, safe, alternatives to membership in the "club."

Another story: in 1994, I attended the United Nations Conference on Population and Development in Cairo, Egypt. The previous year there had been the United Nations Earth Summit conference in Rio. I was there and so was Bella Abzug and a whole lot of women. The thing is, though, that the women weren't part of the official delegation where the Plans of Action that result from these international conferences are drawn up. Apparently, women, like all the other non-governmental organizations, were viewed as a special interest group that didn't really have a place at the table.

Bella and her army of women began to study how the United Nations worked—where were the cracks and crevices, and how could they widen them and get themselves inside the next time?

The next time was the Cairo conference and its purpose was to figure out how to create sustainable development and stabilize population growth. The previous such conferences, like the one in Mexico City, had had Plans of Action written by men and female ventriloquists for the patriarchy and they focused on contraception and quotas.

Bella, by now, had figured out the UN. She had mobilized her troops, she had the support of a powerful but vagina-friendly man named Tim Wirth, former Colorado senator.

For the first time in the history of such UN conferences, women were organized and at the table, drafting the Plan of Action. These were women from all over the world. One hundred eighty-four countries were represented. They were the women who lived this issue of population and development. They were the front-line workers. The entire organizing aegis for the conference was gender. The message was, "If you want to eradicate poverty and create sustainable development, you—the World Bank, the International Monetary Fund, the United States Agency for International Development and all other governments and

NGOs—you have to view everything you do through a gender lens: Does your project help women and girls? Does it make their lives easier? Does it empower them? Is your structural adjustment scheme going to make it harder for women to get loans to start their own businesses? Is your proposed dam going to make it harder for girls to fetch water for their families?

Everywhere in the developing world it is women and girls who plant the seeds, till the land, harvest the crops, fetch the water, cook the food, bear the children, take charge of the family's health, spend whatever monies they can scrape up on the family's well-being. They are already stretched to their human limits and beyond. Make it worse for them and everything gets worse. Make it easier for them and everything gets better.

You want to reduce population growth, you have to stop thinking about contraception alone. Contraception is vital but it's not enough. In some places, if a woman tries to use contraception she risks being beaten or even killed. In other places she needs all the children she can bear in order to have any status at all, in order to have enough hands to do all the work.

So—do you *really* want to reduce population growth? Try educating girls. Educated girl don't want big families, they can read the labels on medicine bottles, they have the confidence to talk to the male doctors and really understand about heath risks.

Help girls and women start businesses or become wage earners. I visited a non-governmental organization in Cairo that teaches the daughters of the city's garbage collectors (who live in the most unspeakable poverty) how to make things out of recycled garbage and it earns them $17 a month. When a girl brings home even this paltry amount, everything changes; the parents suddenly see that perhaps the girl is worthy to go to school after all. The girl feels empowered enough to say, "No, I will not be married off at thirteen to someone of your choice. I want to finish school, get a better job and marry who I like . . . and I don't want a lot of children." The simple fact of earning an income changes everything. That, of course, is why the same mind-set that opposes a woman's right to reproductive freedom also opposes women working. Both of those are battles about power—not about the personhood of the fetus.

The year after the Cairo conference, there was the UN Women's Conference in Beijing, China. I was there, too. And I returned the following year to visit family planning clinics and was told that the conference had had a profound effect on women in China who hadn't even been to the conference. "Why?" I asked, and it was explained to me that the statement "Women's rights are human rights" had leaked out and spread around the country and Chinese women had received this like, "Oh, my God! Our rights are human rights." It had never occurred to them.

Okay. I carry within me now, all these stories and more, these concrete examples of what it means for the planet to move to the feminine. I *need* these things within me—I *need* to understand, for instance, that the entire framework of psychology up until the 1970s was based on a male-centered definition of what is normal and, as a result, women end up feeling there is something terribly wrong with our more relational, more *feeling* way of doing and seeing. Finally, our way is validated, put into a theoretical framework by this new wave of women psychologists.

I *need* to own this. You know why? For the times when patriarchy attacks and makes the criticisms that we are so vulnerable to. Hey, the Male Role Belief System hasn't been around this long because it's stupid. Well, it *is* stupid, but it's not dumb—it knows our Achilles heel: "Oh, those women, they're so fuzzy-headed, so impractical, so out of touch, so lacking in strategy." And we internalize that and think it's true, but it's *not* true. We all need to hold that inside our bodies, have it anchored within us by our own examples, by our own stories that remind us that what is going to save people everywhere in the world is moving away from the paradigm that "might makes right" and that "power is all," to the balanced yin and yang, love, compassion and forgiveness existing along with the male qualities of efficiency, goal orientation and strength. No one can deny what patriarchy has done to our earth.

We have to understand that it is a *belief system* that is the enemy, not men. We have to understand that empathy is revolutionary—empathy for women, for men, for ourselves. We need to work to create a movement that is like a volcano which will erupt when the time is right, in a flow of soft, hot, empathic, breathing, authentic, vagina-friendly, relational lava that will circle patriarchy and smother it so that men and women, boys and girls, can be whole again, head and heart united.